MORE STORIES OF SOUTHAMPTON STREETS

By

A.G.K. Leonard

Published by Paul Cave Publications Ltd.
74 Bedford Place, Southampton

Printed by Brown and Son (Ringwood) Ltd.

I.S.B.N. 0-86146-074-X
Published: 1989

CONTENTS

Introduction

This book is a sequel to *Stories of Southampton Streets*, published in 1984. These further explorations of aspects of local history and biography clarify the origins of more Southampton street and road names, whose significance has often become blurred or forgotten over the years.

By enduring personal association or specific commemorative intent, many such names exemplify phases in the history of Southampton and serve as "memorials" of those who in various ways contributed to its development. The people whose names and homes are perpetuated on the local street scene may not all be "celebrities" but in this context they are all worth recalling.

Some impinged only briefly on Southampton — like John William Newcombe of Market Harborough, whose biography is outlined in relation to Edwardian house building in the Polygon area, and William Winn, who gave his name to the road that saw the most select of late Victorian "villa" development. Previously, there have been only vague references to the presumed connection of Winn Road with "a certain Mr. Winn": I have been able to document it and discover something of the — somewhat surprising — background of "William Winn Esq., of Haddo House, Bow, Middlesex".

More deeply rooted in Southampton was John Butler Harrison, who lived until 1850 in the house off St. Mary Street he bought in 1789: his name soon became attached to the lane running beside his garden — Harrison's Cut is still on the street map two centuries later.

By contrast, Ogle Road was a late Victorian creation across the site of a town "mansion" occupied from 1792 by members of the family after whom it was named — although the property itself can be traced back to Tudor times.

Many other byways of local history are explored in this book, in relation to the changing scene at the Polygon and the mainly Victorian development as residential suburbs of former "country house" estates like Bellevue, Freemantle and Shirley.

The chapters are self-contained but some of their stories link with others told in my previous book, to which (abbreviated as *Streets*) references are therefore made in the text where necessary to avoid repetition.

The interest of the areas surveyed in this book is often historical and topographical rather than architectural but the present townscape includes some attractive survivals of a more leisured and "genteel" age and streets of evocative period character. As a guide for walks around them and as a help in recognising the outlines of former estates, there is the excellent Ordnance Survey *Southampton City Map* — large-scale and very clear, with a comprehensive index of city streets.

There are, of course, many more Southampton streets which in one way or another commemorate or recall individuals as diverse as builders, surveyors, engineers, shopkeepers, market gardeners and many others, as well as royalty and national heroes, both military and political. A third book will be needed to tell their stories . . .

In writing of Southampton streets, I use the words "street" and "road" almost interchangeably, with the former taken to include the latter and its modern variants. "Street" is the old name for a built-up thoroughfare, deriving from the Roman *via strata*, i.e., a paved way. A "road" was originally a highway, along which travellers rode their horses from one place to another.

"Streets" are now identified with "down-town" areas of business premises or rows of smaller and older houses, whereas from Victorian times a "road" address has carried more attractive suburban and "out of town" associations. The older "genteel" street synonyms of Place, Square, Crescent, Terrace and Villas have given way to others like Gardens, Avenue, Drive, Grove, Way, Walk, Court and Close — all variously favoured by developers seeking a distinctive designation for rows of new houses.

The latest "in" word on the housing scene seems to be "Mews" — now applied to almost any group of suburban or "town" houses with "up-market" aspirations.

It was the old word for sets of stables arranged around a yard, originally deriving from the royal stables at Charing Cross, built where the royal hawks once mewed, i.e., moulted. Later, side streets thus known as mews were built in London for the stables and coach houses of the nobility and gentry living in nearby squares and terraces. Sometimes coachmen and stable boys lived there, "over the job". As horses were superseded, the mews premises were converted into private dwellings, which themselves became fashionable.

In Southampton, new houses between Pointout Road and Burgess Road have been styled Hode Stone Mews, harking back to the ancient boundary marker. The Hode Stone Cross, which in Tudor times marked the north-west corner of the Common, stood in what is now Upper Hill Lane, originally on the east side between present Rockstone and Highclere Roads. More recently, its surviving base was moved to the opposite side of the road, where a modern tablet identifies it: its earlier position is marked by a metal stud.

It is now well outside the Common, having been by-passed when travellers took a short cut across the top corner, creating the trackway that became Burgess Street, i.e., the highway of the burgesses or citizens. This was renamed Burgess Road in 1924, presumably for greater residential "gentility". It became the accepted boundary of the Common, with the section north of it "lost" to the townsfolk when the main area was enclosed with earth banks in Elizabethan times. The Boundary Commissioners of 1835 even detached this "point-out" from the borough, to which it was not restored until the extension of 1920.

Whatever the variations on the word "street" and whether they be modern creations inspired by historical associations or enduring survivals from earlier times, the street names of Southampton recall and exemplify aspects of its history, linking past and present in ways that can easily be overlooked. Some of the stories behind these names are presented in the following chapters.

The plaque at the Polygon Hotel commemorating its role as U.S. Army headquarters during World War II. (Photograph: Tom Holder).

The Polygon in 1783, from a contemporary engraving.

The Polygon and all that

Why is The Polygon so called? To those unfamiliar with its history, it must seem curious that a stretch of road, an hotel and a school, together with the largely Edwardian residential area around them, all carry a name, from the Greek, meaning a many-sided figure. This classical identity, originating some 220 years ago, derives from a grandiose but abortive project to create an aristocratic "garden suburb" on the then outskirts of Southampton during its short heyday as a spa and resort town in Georgian times.

Southampton was saved from a continuation of its earlier commercial decline by the advent of fashionable visitors seeking the benefits of "taking the waters" — both by sea-bathing and by drinking the outflow of a chalybeate spring, to which all manner of medical virtues were ascribed. The town's new role was fostered by royal patronage, initiated by Frederick, Prince of Wales, who visited it in 1750 and found the sea water "salubrious and invigorating". The Corporation hastened to elect him as an honorary burgess, presenting him with "a copy of his freedom of the town in a gold box" — which cost £35.11s.6d. The Prince died a few months later (of pleurisy, after catching a chill playing tennis) but his sons the Dukes of York, Cumberland and Gloucester maintained the association with Southampton, which by 1781 could boast more royal burgesses than any other town. More significantly, from a mere 3,000 around 1750, its population grew by some 50 per cent, during the third quarter of the century and rose again to nearly 8,000 by its end.

In the 1760s, Southampton was expanding and reconstructing as a watering place, providing hotels, lodgings "fitted up in the neatest and genteelest manner", coffee houses and circulating libraries; fashionable shops in the High Street and elegant new houses in Above Bar; bathing establishments and assembly rooms, notably Martin's Baths and Long Room on the West Quay; a theatre in French Street, the "Beach" promenade eastwards from the Platform, and, of course, the Spa Gardens (in the area of the later Spa Road: the original stone fountain can be seen in Tudor House Museum). Although the Corporation built a new Audit House that enhanced the High Street scene from 1773, services like street lighting and paving lagged behind these developments and patrons of the Long Rooms, Baths and Theatre suffered inconvenience, sometimes injury, when passing through the squalid, unlit and undrained side streets and lanes, too narrow for carriages — hence the proliferation of sedan chairs.

Southampton was nevertheless esteemed for its pleasant situation and surroundings, where country houses and villas started to ring the town. In 1768 an ambitious project was conceived to provide a new "assemblage of elegant edifices" on a commanding site north of the walls, to offer a more "select" setting for residence and social functions than the town itself then provided.

The main promoters were a local man of property, Isaac Mallortie, and General John Carnac. Coming from a Dublin family of Huguenot extraction, Carnac had followed a military career that took him to India in 1754: when his regiment was posted home in 1758, he preferred to remain there, transferring to the service of the East India Company, in which he distinguished himself and became closely associated with Robert Clive — "the person to whom I owe everything". Carnac returned to England with Clive in 1767 and applied some of his Indian wealth to buying an estate at Cams Hall, near Fareham, where the architect Jacob Leroux remodelled the mansion for him.

He got himself elected M.P. for Leominster, for which he sat in the Parliaments of 1768-74. His speeches dealt mainly with Indian affairs: in one, he declared "I have not a shilling that causes me to blush . . . had I been rapacious I might have had four times the fortune I have". Clive had earlier pressed the East India Company directors to allow Carnac to accept the "presents" (worth £32,000 then and equivalent to several millions in today's money) given by the Mogul and the Rajah of Benares, when they made peace with the company in 1765; he wrote "I found him the only officer of rank who had resisted the temptations to which, by his station, he was constantly subject, of acquiring an immense fortune". Carnac evidently had problems getting his wealth transferred to England but he had enough on hand to invest in the development of the Polygon.

Carnac and Mallortie enlisted the services of Jacob Leroux, an established London architect, to design a striking layout for the site described in Baker's *Southampton Guide* as comprising "about twenty-two acres of fine gravelly soil, which being agreeably elevated, commanded a most delightful prospect of Southamton Water as far as Calshot Castle, with fine views of the New Forest and the town of Southampton, as well as many gentlemen's seats, and a distant view of the Isle of Wight".

The curve of modern Handel Terrace and The Polygon represents a section of the carriage drive around the original site of The Polygon, for which Leroux planned twelve large houses, facing outwards, with the gardens behind them tapering back like spokes of a wheel to "a large bason of water in the middle". Adjacent to this grouping, the scheme also included "a capital building with two detached wings and colonades, of which the centre was an elegant tavern, with assembly and card rooms etc., and each wing was an hotel to accommodate the nobility and gentry".

Set in the wall of the present Polygon Hotel, left of its main entrance, is the foundation stone of its forerunner. The inscription, recut and outlined in black, records that "This stone (being the first of the Polygon) was Placed ye 9th of Augst. 1768 By The Rt. Honble. Lord Viscount Palmerston and The Rt. Honble. Hans Stanley of Poulton". They were the town's two M.P.s, the

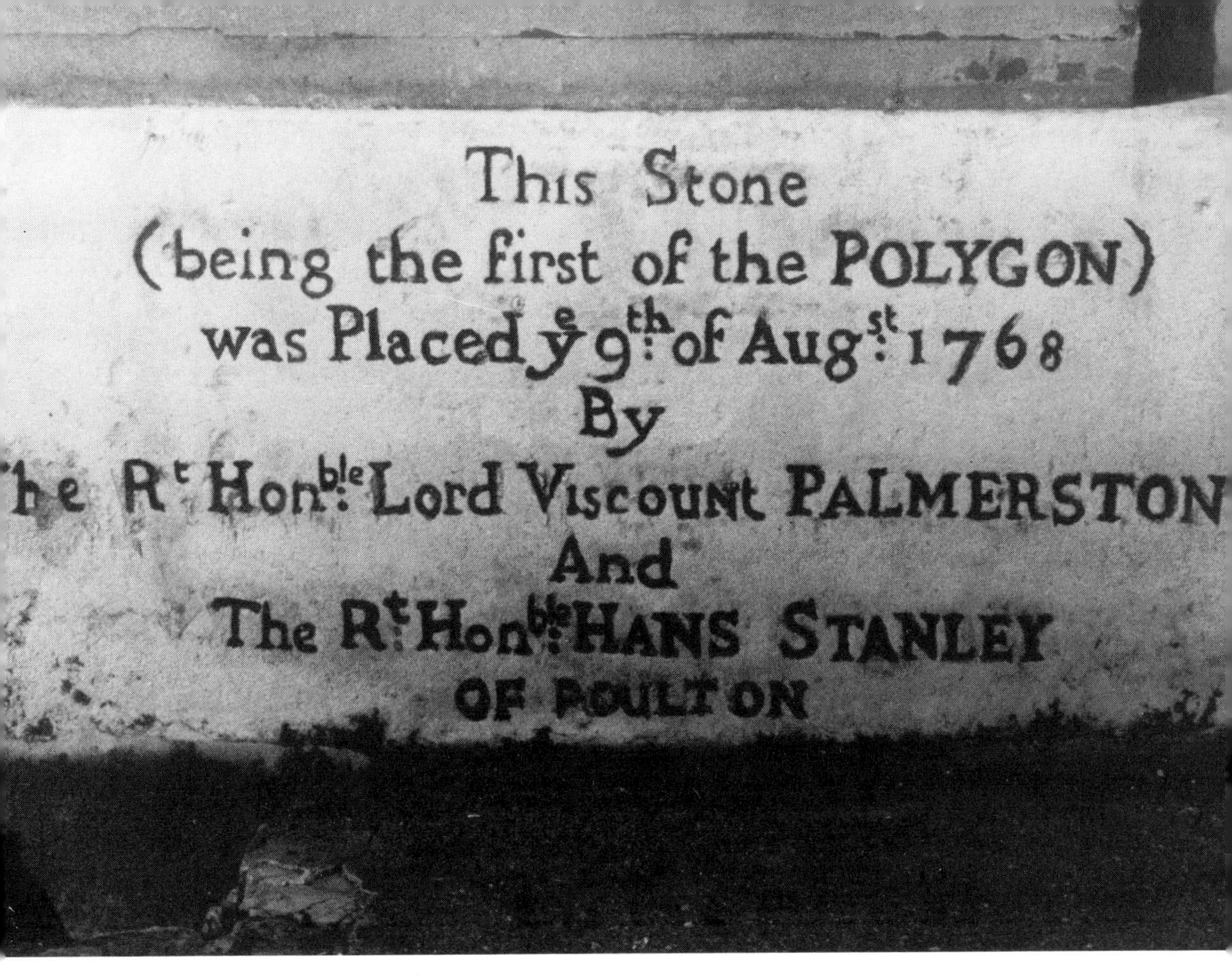

The original foundation stone of the Polygon, 1768. (Photograph: Tom Holder).

former being the father of the Victorian statesman memorialised a century later in the park off Above Bar.

Construction of the Polygon must have proceeded quickly enough at first, as evidenced by a letter written in August 1771 by Mrs. James Harris to her son, later the first Earl of Malmesbury, describing her visit "to see the new building called the Polygon". She wrote "'tis a fine thing and every house has a most beautiful view of the sea and the town of Southampton. There is a most magnificent hotel, in which there is a fine ballroom, card, tea and two billiard-rooms, several eating rooms and they say fifty good bedchambers and stabling for 500 horses. There are to be all sorts of elegant shops in this hotel; at present there is only a jeweller and a hairdresser. I never saw so great a preparation both for luxury and elegance".

The hotel was then being run by a Mr. Frere, who staged weekly "Dressed Balls" — intended to out-class other assemblies at the Long Rooms and the Dolphin, where townsfolk, even some "in trade", were liable to lower the social tone.

As Mrs. Harris noted, "some make exceptions to the distance. Frere, to obviate that, has sent to London for three new coaches, which will carry ladies there at threepence a head". Another visitor of 1771, Mrs. Constantia Orlebar, described the Polygon as "a large handsome Building for the Reception of Company, a mile from the town and a pretty drive from thence".

Carriages and sedan chairs were needed by Polygon patrons lodging in the town; to walk there was hazardous on account of the lack of street lighting beyond Above Bar and the risk of assault or robbery, as instanced by a *Hampshire Chronicle* report in September, 1773 — "A young gentleman, a stranger to the town, attempted to walk from his lodgings to the hall in his mask, dressed in the character of a shepherd, but the mob insulted him greatly by throwing him down and tossing him like a football for some time and, in all probability, would have ended his life if some humane persons had not interrupted them".

The "Great House at the Polygon" was taken on a 30 year lease by the "celebrated Madame Cornelys" who came to Southampton in June, 1773 to begin her brief reign as "the Empress of Taste". The advertised opening for July 29 had to be set back because fittings from London were not completed in time: after announcements that "it will be opened with all convenient speed", the first assembly was held on August 23, towards the end of the summer season. London retailers of perfumes and jewels opened shops in the Polygon and M. Asselin, first dancer of the London Opera House, took up residence to give lessons in "minuets, country dances, cotillons, quadrille, allemande etc". Weekly assemblies were held during the autumn, under the patronage of two royal dukes.

In September a Masked Ball took place "at the particular request of some persons of distinction". Tickets at a guinea made it exclusive but "not very crowded" and the occasion was marred by some ill-disposed person hurling a large stone through a window, nearly hitting the Duke and Duchess of Gloucester.

Meanwhile, misfortune had struck the Polygon promoters. Mallortie was declared bankrupt in July and his assets were put up for sale. Having unsuccessfully begged Warren Hastings to use his influence "to get a part or the whole of his fortune sent him by every opportunity", Carnac was obliged to return to India, where he decided to remain. He sold his Cams Hall estate to the Delmes family in 1781 and spent the rest of his life in India, dying at Bangalore in 1800, aged 84. Carnac and Mallortie had occupied two of the only three houses then completed at the Polygon. When they left, no-one seemed willing to take over the project.

Jacob Leroux had exhibited a view of his Polygon scheme at the Royal Academy in 1771, followed in 1772 by his "design for a public chapel and shops, forming a forum, intended to be built at the Polygon, Southampton".

This never got beyond his drawing board. Leroux cherished his Polygon concept for another twenty years, however, and returned to it in 1793 when — as a speculative builder as well as architect, as was not uncommon in those days — he planned a similar layout on the Somers estate in north London, for 32 houses arranged around a figure having fifteen sides, instead of twelve as intended at Southampton. Again, his hopes were disappointed. The London project seemed to prosper initially but then "some unforeseen causes occurred which checked the fervour of building and many carcases of houses were sold for less than the value of the materials". His Georgian mansions eventually gave way to a late Victorian block of flats, styled Polygon Buildings.

In another context, Leroux was the subject of a bitter reference by Charles Dibdin, the celebrated Southampton-born composer of nautical songs like "Tom Bowling" (there is a memorial tablet to him at the ruined Holy Rood church, of which his father was the parish clerk). In his "Musical Tour", published in 1788, Dibdin wrote of losing £290 "by building a castle in the air near Pancras, by virtue of an agreement with the famous — I had almost added another syllable — Jacob Leroux Esq., architect, brick-maker and trading justice in the district of Clerkenwell". Dibdin felt himself the victim of "this gentleman's dastardly speciousness for which a hyena might envy him" in a sequence of events which ended with the skeleton of his house being blown down by a high wind.

At Southampton, Mrs. Cornelys withdrew from her Polygon lease and advertisements in May, 1774, failed to attract a successor. The London perfumer Thevenot re-opened his shop at the Polygon, offering "the best powder, foreign pomatum, essences, perfume water of all kinds . . . ladies' purses, scented bags, garters, foreign wash-balls and the new invented Italian soap, with directions" and another programme of balls and concerts was somehow arranged for the reason — patronised by the Duke and Duchess of Cumberland, who rented Mallortie's former house.

The season ended in late September with a "Grand Ball and Supper given by the noblemen and gentlemen to the ladies who particularly honour and grace this place with their rank and beauty". Although well attended, this occasion nevertheless signalised the end of the Polygon as what might now be called an "up-market leisure complex". At that time, it was indeed "too far out of town": the coach-owning nobility, other "carriage folk" and hotel patrons were not numerous enough to make the Polygon viable as the major focus of Southampton's social scene during its "spa period".

Soon afterwards, the central "tavern" and colonnades were demolished and the two hotel wings were converted into "convenient and elegant dwellings". A few more large houses were subsequently built in the south-east section of the Polygon and to the north of it. Further building proceeded piecemeal, on a more modest scale, and by the 1830s the guidebooks were describing the area as "a situation much resorted to by families of respectability and eminence" — subtly distinguished in these terms from the "nobility and gentry" for whom the abortive project of 1768-74 was planned to cater.

From the 1780s, successive editions of Baker's *Southampton Guide* lamented "could the plan have been completed, it would be one of the first places in the kingdom, perhaps in the world, regarded in the view of modern architecture". They did not fail to mention the Polygon's surviving amenity: "the exterior part is encircled with a fine gravel road which is much frequented by company in carriages and otherwise" — "otherwise" presumably alluding to its popularity as a promenade for courting couples.

The whole aspect of the area changed in Edwardian times, when it became "ripe for development" as a suburb of the expanding town and was soon covered with semi-detached villas and terraces. In the stretch of road that now alone carries the name of the vanished Polygon (parts of the former Polygon Road leading down from Bedford Place were redesignated Henstead and Devonshire Roads in 1921) a neat group of four "listed" houses survives from the 1840s, still displaying traces of "gentility" with attractive little balconies, canopy and railings. One of the large old houses of the original Polygon became an hotel again around the turn of the century; unlike its forerunner, the present Polygon Hotel has flourished steadily, having been rebuilt in 1937-38 (when a single room with private bath could be had for 11s.6d a night) and further extended and modernised in post-war years.

North of the hotel, parts of the former Polygon Road were supplanted by Handel Terrace and Handel Road, built up from 1908 onwards. George Frederick Handel, born in Saxony in 1685, came to England in 1710 and soon won fame for his operas and oratorios: acknowledgements of his musical genius ranged from appointment as official court composer in 1727 to burial in Westminster Abbey in 1759. There is, however, more to the origin of the Handel street names than a simple compliment to the man who carried choral music to its highest level, for they relate to Handel College, the private boys' school conducted for nearly fifty years by Aaron Harvey and his son Frank. The elder Harvey was himself a talented musician and music featured prominently in the curriculum of his school, signalised by the name he chose for it.

Born in 1835, son of a Somerset mining engineer, Aaron Harvey has passed out top of his year at Highbury Training College. He came to Southampton in 1858, as headmaster of the boys' department of All Saints school (opened ten years previously at York Buildings, taken over by the School Board from the church authorities in 1882 and closed in 1931, when the vacated building served as a Dockland Settlement until bombed in 1940). At the end of 1863

Opposite: The Polygon area as shown on the town map issued by I.T. Lewis in 1843.

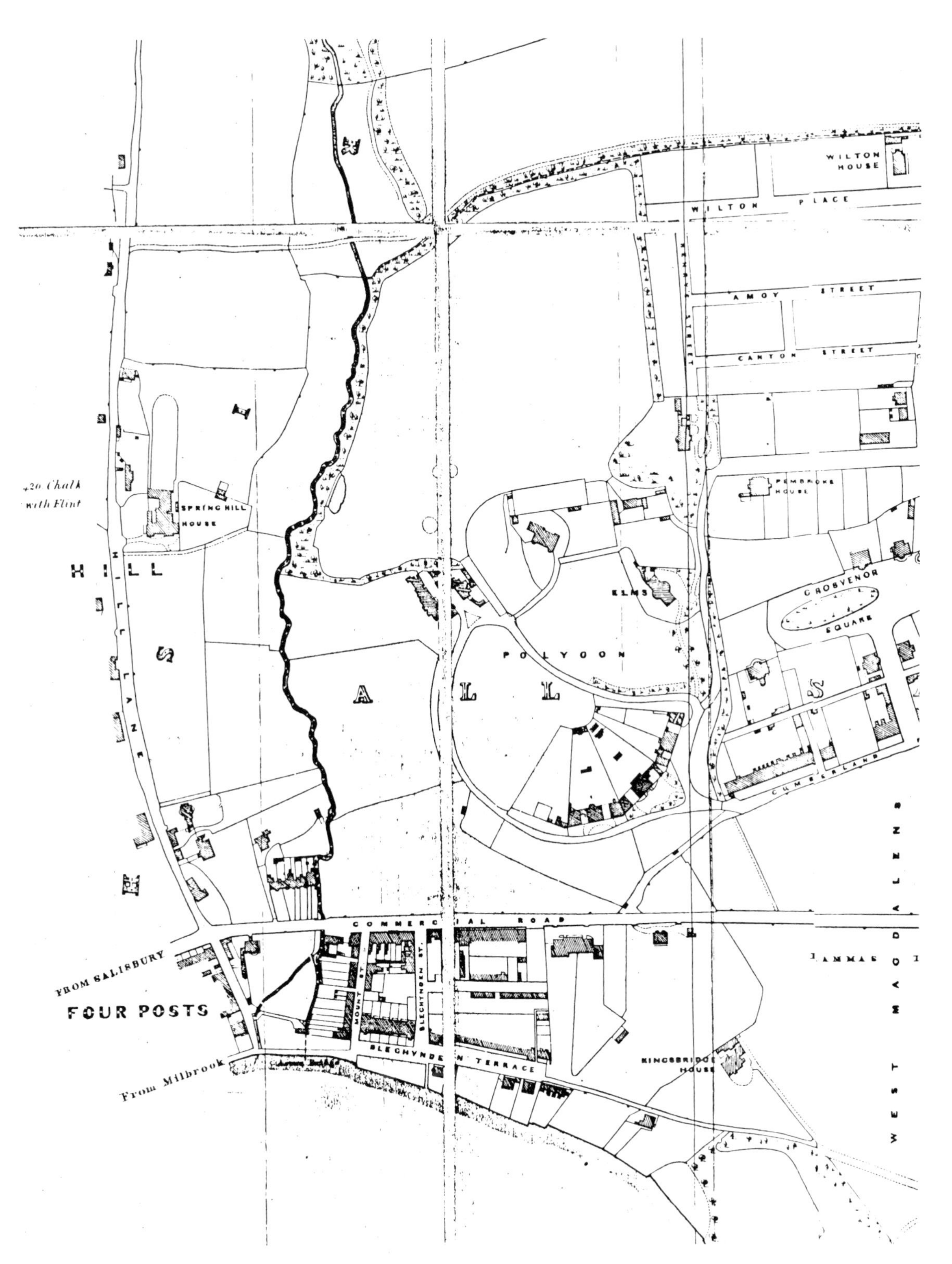
WILTON HOUSE
WILTON PLACE
AMOY STREET
CANTON STREET
PEMBROKE HOUSE
420 Chalk with Flint
SPRING HILL HOUSE
HILL
GROSVENOR SQUARE
ELMS
POLYGON
A L L
S
CUMBERLAND
COMMERCIAL ROAD
LAMMAS
FROM SALISBURY
FOUR POSTS
MOUNT ST.
BLECHYNDEN ST.
BLECHYNDEN TERRACE
KINGSBRIDGE HOUSE
From Milbrook
WEST MAGDALENS

Harvey received "a magnificent timepiece" from a testimonial subscription when he left All Saints to set up his own school at his house in Anglesea Place and later Lower Prospect Place, Above Bar. He was prominent in the musical life of the town, as conductor of the Southampton Philharmonic Society and organist and choirmaster at St. Peter's church. Aaron Harvey retired in 1895, when his son Frank took over the school, in which he had previously assisted his father, but the latter continued teaching music and running the school orchestra up to his death in 1905.

Rev. Frank Northam Harvey (1864-1939) took holy orders in 1889 after graduating from Oxford. He spent three years as a curate at St. Denys before devoting himself primarily to Handel College — although still making time to serve from 1894 to 1910 as chaplain at the Royal South Hants Hospital, with which he always maintained a close connection. In 1897 he transferred Handel College from Above Bar to the Polygon, where Polygon Lodge became the family home, with the school itself occupying another large old house on the outer side (the site of Sembal House), with playing fields nearby. The headmaster added sporting strengths to Handel College, particularly in cricket.

He himself was a good enough batsman/wicket-keeper to play three first class matches for Hampshire in 1899-1900. For one of them he adopted the pseudonym F.H. Northam, which later led to him appearing twice in the official history of the County club — with which he continued actively involved as a committee member right up to his death.

Handel College offered a broad curriculum and a lively range of activities. Although there were never more than a hundred boys, they could field a football team to beat the Hartley College students. Old Handelian dinners exemplified the high standing of the College. In 1900 Aaron Harvey was presented with a testimonial portrait by a former pupil, Leonard Skates (1874-1943), then making his name as an artist of some distinction. Presiding on this occasion was another notable "old boy", George Hussey (1864-1950) who in his thirties was mayor of Southampton for three successive years, 1898-1900, and was knighted in 1901.

In the *Handelian* of April 1907 the headmaster reported the acquisition of a replacement playing field — "one that has so far escaped the desecrating hand of the builders. Such a maze of red houses has sprung up in the Polygon during these last twelve months that Old Handelians would need a guide to find the school". In 1910 Rev. F.N. Harvey decided it was time to give up his school. He spent the next 14 years as vicar of Whitchurch and then served as rector of Fawley for another ten years until 1934. Returning to live in Banister Gardens, he enjoyed an active retirement that included winters abroad as chaplain to British visitors in Portugal and France.

Handel College was briefly run by A. Heriz Smith in 1910-11 but from January 1912 its "large and commodious premises, 100 ft. above sea level, with

Hurst Leigh School (previously Handel College) from a postcard issued by the school about 1913.

Hurst Leigh School – the boys' senior classroom, about 1913.

good view of Southampton Water, convenient to trams and railway station, well drained, standing in about an acre of ground" were taken over by Hurst Leigh School. This "high class modern preparatory school for boys and girls" had been established in 1909 by Lionel Caulfeild, M.A. ("Late Inspector of Education, South Africa") and his wife at 51 Archers Road — the house at the Hill Lane end, then called "Glenfinnart", which later became the Winston Hotel. When this proved too small for its expanding numbers of day and boarding pupils, Caulfeild took the opportunity to transfer his school to the solid old three-storey square block at the Polygon, which, after renovation, was advertised as "an ideal spot for children, with its large airy classrooms, high situation and three acres of grounds" — two of them as private playing fields nearby. Caulfeild ran his school there until 1936, afterwards continuing to take pupils at his house in Hill Lane for several more years.

Morris Road, running diagonally through the old Polygon lands from Commercial Road to Devonshire Road, was laid out and built up in 1907-10. It was named in compliment to Richard William Morris, who lived for many years at the old Georgian house called "The Elms", which stood south of the junction of Morris and Devonshire Roads. It took its name from the avenue of elms lining part of Polygon/Devonshire Road, planted to enhance the drive around the Polygon as originally envisaged. In late Victorian times this section was known as Elms Road but the name lost significance when most of the old trees were blown down by a gale in 1898.

Directories show R.W. Morris living at "The Elms" from 1870 to 1904. Little is now known of him, beyond the fact that he was evidently of "independent means" — listed under "nobility and gentry" with no indication of his profession or occupation. "The Elms" seems to have stood empty for some years, after his death or removal. It was last listed in 1910, as 69 Polygon Road, then the home of Charles Wheeler. The house must have been demolished shortly afterwards, to give way to smaller scale residential development.

There was a curious echo of the Polygon past in 1923, when house owners in the section of Devonshire Road between Henstead and Handel Roads objected to paying for private street works on the grounds that it was "an ancient highway, repairable by the inhabitants at large". The corporation argued it was a private road, which it had never repaired. Evidence was given that until removed in 1914 when the road was widened by the local authority, there was a gate at the south end of the road, closed one day a year to maintain its private status. The magistrates resolved the dispute by requiring the frontagers to pay 60 per cent of the road charges, with the corporation itself meeting the balance.

Although their significance may now pass unrecognised, Newcombe and Harborough Roads combine to perpetuate the surname and home town of the enterprising property developer responsible for laying out with Edwardian

Early Victorian houses at The Polygon. (Photograph: Tom Holder).

houses both the Polygon area and the Terrace House estate to the north of it — John William Newcombe (1856-1924), of Market Harborough.

Moving to that Leicestershire town from the nearby Northamptonshire village of Clipston, where his family was long established, he entered an auctioneer-surveyor's office at 14 and trained in accountancy. In 1875, not yet twenty, he started his own business as a house and property agent, in association with his brother Arthur. Four years later, J.W. Newcombe became secretary of the infant Market Harborough Building Society, which he energetically served and guided for the next 44 years of solid growth. From developing sites for house building in Market Harborough (giving it a Newcombe Street), he extended his own activities to various Midland towns, in partnership with his brother and Samuel Symington — better known as a dealer in coffee and soups. Formation of the Newcombe Estates Company in 1905 brought in further capital for expansion to London suburbs and towns like Southampton.

Beginning in 1905 by buying land at the Polygon, the company soon seized the opportunity to acquire the adjoining Terrace House estate. Fronting 23 acres of grounds extending from Devonshire to Burlington Road and northwards to the old "Fitzhugh path" running between the backs of the houses of present-day Wilton Avenue and Milton Road, Terrace House itself occupied approximately the site of the Central Baptist Church, at the junction of Kenilworth and Devonshire Roads. From 1860 the mansion — then "out of town" but still at a convenient carriage drive distance from Northam — was the home of Charles Arthur Day, second generation co-principal of the shipbuilding firm Day, Summers and Co. His widow remained at Terrace House until her death in 1905, after which the property was put up for sale.

Disposal of this "valuable freehold residential and building estate" was handled in London by Edwin Fox and Bousefield, who sold it by auction on May 16, 1906 as "The Mart, Tokenhouse Yard, Bank of England". Their particulars described the "substantial residence" as including a double drawing room, detached billiard room, a five-room bachelor wing, five principal and four servants' bedrooms, servants' hall and extensive basements, with two wine cellars, along with gardens, lawns, range of glass houses, stabling for seven horses, "model farmery" and standing for seven cows, plus three well-built cottages. Echoing the interests of the former owner (who had been a familiar figure in his scarlet coat riding horse until well into his seventies), the auctioneers noted that "the sporting facilities in the immediate neighbourhood include three packs of foxhounds and the New Forest staghounds within easy reach; golf links are near at hand, whilst for yachting there are unrivalled opportunities".

Yet they can hardly have envisaged Terrace House continuing as a private residence; although "well adapted for a public institution", it ranked a poor second to the "immediate building capabilities" of the 23 acres "with frontages to existing roads and affording great facilities for profitable development . . . so circumstanced as to make the formation of several other thoroughfares an early and profitable operation. The situation, means of access and general configuration, together with the continually increasing demand in this locality for moderate sized houses, render the immediate development of the property imperative and any well devised scheme for dealing with the estate, either by building, resale in plots or creation of ground rents, is sure to be attended with successful results".

These Newcombe's company evidently achieved over the next few years, laying out roads and services (using its own works department) and disposing of house plots to builders and individuals. J.W. Newcombe assisted the building on his land of the Baptist church, to which the congregation started at East

John William Newcombe (1856-1924).

Street in 1689 transferred in 1910. He provided the site at a rebate of 100 guineas and contributed similarly to the church building fund. Set into its walls is the stone he laid on April 6, 1910. Three years previously, he had officially opened the new building of Market Harborough Baptist church, of which he and his brother Arthur were zealous members and generous supporters — the latter as secretary, the former as treasurer for 22 years until his death in 1924. J.W. Newcombe was for many years president of local Free Church councils, a county J.P. and an active Liberal.

The Market Harborough estate agents J.W. and A. Newcombe lost their separate identity in 1970 but the Newcombe Estates Company continued, centred in London: its board preserved family continuity, with the founder's eldest son, Mr. Reginald Newcombe, as long-serving chairman from 1930 and his two sons as managing directors. The Newcombe company kept links with Southampton, holding investment property in the city, while between the wars it was responsible for housing developments along the Millbrook Road, at Maybush and at Bitterne.

The roads laid out by the company across the Terrace House estate included two named Coventry and Kenilworth, reflecting its Midlands connections. "Kenilworth" also echoed the title of Sir Walter Scott's popular novel, based on the tradition of Amy Robsart, wife of Queen Elizabeth's favourite the Earl of Leicester, meeting a tragic death at his castle there. This literary association prompted one of the more remarkable but lesser-known features of the Southampton townscape — the portrait gallery in stone of ten famous men of letters which adorns the fronts of five pairs of semi-detached villas on the south side of Kenilworth Road.

These finely detailed relief portraits were carved in Bath stone by a craftsman well known in Southampton during the first four decades of this century, Charles Henry Meadows. For twenty years he worked for the old-established firm of monumental masons, Garret and Haysom, who provided these unusual decorations for the builder, believed to have been F. and J. Young, then operating from Clovelly Road. From the front walls of the houses in Kenilworth Road (even numbers 4-22) ten portrait heads look out from below the sills of the bedroom windows, arranged in pairs, each with distinctive surrounds of floral decorations, scrolls and swags.

The medallions on numbers 4 and 6 frame the familiar features of William Shakespeare and the blind poet John Milton. Two bearded heads adorn the fronts of numbers 8 and 10, where Alfred, first Baron Tennyson, appointed Poet Laureate in 1850, is flanked by the prolific novelist Charles Dickens. Looking towards each other over the front room windows of numbers 12 and 14 are two Scotsmen. The first is Sir Walter Scott (1771-1832), author of many historical novels besides "Kenilworth", along with numerous other literary, dramatic, poetical and antiquarian works. His companion in stone is Robert Burns (1759-1796), whose verses are still much quoted and sung. A more disparate pair of literary "lions" appear on the next two house fronts: their bearded features are those of Thomas Carlyle (No. 16) and Henry Longfellow (No. 18). Carlyle (1795-1881) enjoyed Victorian celebrity as essayist, historian and lecturer but is now less remembered than Longfellow (1807-82) — the only American in the Kenilworth Road display of literary sculptures. He was a Harvard professor, widely travelled in Europe, whose works included such well-loved poems as "The Wreck of the Hesperus" and "Hiawatha".

"The Sculptor", a painting by Edward Greig of C.H. Meadows at work.
(Courtesy Southampton Art Gallery).

William Shakespeare.

John Milton.

Lord Tennyson.

Charles Dickens.

Sir Walter Scott.

Robert Burns.

Thomas Carlyle.

Henry Longfellow.

Charles Kingsley.

William Wordsworth.

Literary 'greats' – a portrait gallery in stone. Carvings on the fronts of houses in Kenilworth Road.

(Photographs: Tom Holder).

Not all these stone portraits are generally recognised today but their identities are confirmed by reference to them in an article on the Polygon, written by John D. Haysom and published in the *Southampton Times* of November 20, 1909 — very soon after they had been carved at his Eastgate Masonry Works and fixed in position. Two further carvings, not mentioned in Haysom's article, were shortly afterwards placed on another pair of houses in Kenilworth Road. Their subjects are identified by the sculptor's own annotations on old photographs of his works, now held by his grandson, to whom the writer is indebted for information about C.H. Meadows.

Depicted beneath the bedroom window of number 20 is Charles Kingsley (1819-75); looking towards him from the wall of number 22 is William Wordsworth (1770-1850) the great Lakeland poet, Poet Laureate from 1843. Kingsley spent most of his life as rector of Eversley, serving this scattered parish in north-east Hampshire with dedication, but also involved himself in national movements for social reform and produced a wide range of novels, songs and ballads as well as lectures and sermons. Best known today are his historical novel "Westward Ho!" and his romance for children, "The Water Babies", prompted by his indignation at the exploitation of young boys as chimney sweeps. In Southampton he is memorialised by Kingsley Road, a 1900 development between Foundry Lane and Waterhouse Lane.

Although Morris Road was named after a local resident, transferred association with the artist and writer William Morris (1834-96) may have suggested the decorative features on some of the houses in that road. Four have circular medallions recessed into their front bay walls below the bedroom windows; they contain attractive carved heads but these are stylised character types, not individual portraits. Other houses display generalised and "classical" designs in stone and glazed tiles, some resembling Morris designs.

C.H. Meadows was a talented artist, sculptor and carver in stone and wood, who lived and worked in Southampton for 45 years up to his death in 1942. After studying his crafts in Liverpool (where he was born in 1868) and in London, he came to Southampton in 1897. Before and after World War I he lived in Waterloo Road, Freemantle, then from 1930 at Stafford Road, Shirley. Directories listed him as "C. Henry Meadows, architectural sculptor and carver in marble, stone and wood and moulder in cement". His specialities included elegant wooden scrolls of battle honours for naval vessels and personalised figureheads in traditional style for private yachts — painstakingly fashioned from huge solid blocks of pitch pine into shapes as varied as Chinese dragons and Red Indian warriors, as well as graceful maidens in diverse styles.

His numerous commissions embraced much of the carved stonework for the "Mayflower" memorial and at the Civic Centre, notably the two lions placed outside the Art Gallery and Central Library in 1939. Meadows was saddened when these were smashed by bombs only eighteen months later. A cherished medallion head of his wife, which he had loaned for display at the Art Gallery, was fortunately recovered intact after two days' searching among the wreckage. It remains a family treasure, along with his delicate portrait of the same lady, lovingly drawn in 1897. Meadows' "public" carvings were many and varied, including the lions on the front of the Gaumont (now Mayflower) theatre; the delicate vine patterns on the barge boards of Tudor Buildings in Above Bar; the centrepiece for the children's paddling pool on the Common; and a large figure of Christ in Portland stone for a church at Boscombe. Many more products of his skilful chisel for both public and private memorials now pass without attribution to their sculptor.

Over the years, Meadows contributed to local exhibitions numerous examples of his artistry in smaller scale media — paintings and drawings, models and medallions. Some showed lively humour, imagination and symbolism, others were faithful representations of well-known men, like his plaster relief head of Sir Russell Bencraft (see *Streets*, pages 46-49) and his bust of Colonel Albert W. Swalm, U.S. Consul at Southampton 1903-19, given by his friends to the Avenue Congregational Church to mark his association with it when Avenue Hall served as a rest centre for American and other troops during World War I. Southampton Art Gallery has a plaster low relief, donated in 1940, which Meadows made of the head of George Parker in 1934, only a few months before the death at 90 of this colourful long-haired and bearded character — lifelong temperance campaigner, founder of the Blue Cross choir, town councillor and workhouse Guardian.

The Art Gallery collection also includes a painting "The Sculptor" by Edward Grigg, presented by the artist in 1939, showing Meadows at work, looking a veritable artist in his smock. Meadows was adept with pen and pencil as well as chisel and brush; he delighted to produce a lightning sketch of himself, a distinctively diminutive figure, with moustache and pointed beard, to provide an impromptu "visiting card" when calling at architects' offices.

Half a century before C.H. Meadows was involved in adding artistic distinction to Kenilworth Road, the land between Terrace House and Wilton House had been built up with smaller houses in Amoy and Canton Streets, leading off Bedford Place to dead ends against the boundary wall of the Terrace House grounds. The "cross street" between them became Henry Street, taking the first name of Henry and Henry Joseph Buchan, father and son, the enterprising businessmen who arranged 1,000 year building leases with Rev. William Anthony Fitzhugh, the son and heir of the man who had bought the Banister Court estate in 1792 (see *Streets*, page 9).

Henry Buchan the elder (1794-1865) was a man of wide interests, who contributed purposefully to the artistic and public life of his adopted town, as well as working "to secure for himself a handsome competency" — as Victorian writers liked to describe the financial success of "self-made men". He came to Southampton in 1823 from Portsmouth, where he had set up his own business at the age of twenty. Taking premises in the High Street, Buchan prospered as a high-class house decorator, carver and gilder and also sold glass, picture frames and artists' materials.

His artistic interests and contacts led him to open the Hampshire Picture Gallery in 1827 at 159 High Street, where he offered local artists the use of three well-lit and spacious rooms, open from 7 a.m. to dusk, for the display and sale of their works. Buchan gathered subscriptions and patronage from many Hampshire notables to support this venture — a brave one for a provincial town like Southampton.

Directories of 1836-39 showed Buchan in partnership with a Mr. Slodden but after 1843 the business was styled Buchan and Son, taking in his only son Henry Joseph Buchan (1814-91). Henry Buchan was also prominently involved as promoter or director with the Docks and Itchen Bridge companies, railway projects and the Hampshire Bank, besides actively identifying himself with community activities. He was a long-serving deacon of Above Bar chapel and supporter of the Literary and Philosophical and Mechanics Institutes, Royal British Schools, Royal South Hants Infirmary and various charities. A zealous Liberal, Buchan was first elected a councillor in 1835. Although he later lost his seat, he made a triumphant return in 1847, winning the tiny St. Lawrence ward by one vote to initiate by the same margin his party's control of the borough council for the next 17 years.

In the 1840s Henry Buchan had his home in Orchard Place, then Cranbury Place, before settling at Wilton House — which has survived as the Eye Hospital. He bought this sizeable house in 1845 from John Snook, who had built it in 1831-32. Bedford Place had been built up from the 1820s with a pleasing mixture of sizeable houses and "neat artisans' dwellings" — mostly adapted for commercial purposes as the street became a neighbourhood shopping centre from late Victorian times. The adjoining area was evidently considered "ripe for development" in the 1840s, although this did not materialise as quickly as at first envisaged. Amoy and Canton Streets were named and shown as laid out on the town map "made from actual survey" by I.T. Lewis and published on 1843 but they appeared only in partial outline on the detailed Ordnance Survery map of 1846.

That year Mr. Fitzhugh granted a £2.12s.0d a year building lease for No. 1 Amoy Street, stipulating that the house to be erected there should have "the clear value of at least £150". A house on the south side of Canton Street, near Bedford Place, bears a plaque "Bedford Mews 1837" but the street itself was built up mainly in the 1850s, along with Amoy Street. Compilers of the 1851-53 directories seem to have had difficulties with the name, twice listing "Amour Street" until they got it right from 1855. As Chinese coastal ports, Amoy and Canton should have been familiar in the context of tea clippers and the assertion of British imperial power and trading interests, specifically in the first China War of 1840-42.

This was also known as the Opium War, being occasioned by Chinese efforts to control British traders, whose imports through Canton included large quantities of opium from India. Incidents led to naval and land warfare, in which British forces quickly achieved the "ransom of Canton", the almost bloodless capture of Amoy and the occupation of Shanghai. Hostilities ended when the Chinese agreed to pay heavy compensation to British merchants, give them special trading rights and other privileges and cede Hong Kong to Britain. Queen Victoria's reign saw many such "small wars" as well as larger conflicts: national pride in distant British victories was often expressed in the choice of street names but there seems to have been a more personal element in the naming of Amoy and Canton Streets.

According to the transmitted family memories of a long-time resident in the area, their names were originated by John Snook, the contractor responsible for much of the building in and around Bedford Place, in compliment to two of his sons who were involved in the British operations against China in 1840-42. They, of course, would have been abroad at the time of the 1841 census, when the enumerator recorded John Snook, then 45, with his family, including a son of the same name. Directories showed him living from 1834 — and probably a decade earlier — at Terrace Cottage, a substantial house in Bedford Place on its southern corner with Carlton Place. Census schedules noted Snook as keeping two resident domestic servants: coming from his native Shaftesbury, he had built up a sizeable business in Southampton, for in 1851 he was described as "builder employing 26 men".

He had his own clay pits, brickworks and lime kilns, occupying eleven acres in the area of the present Pointout Road — laid out from 1903 across the former brickfield. Snook is credited with building the Riding School in Carlton Place, which Philip Brannon thought "in every respect the finest building in the kingdom devoted to this purpose": it later served as a Hampshire Volunteers drill hall and was refurbished in 1981 for the Officers Training Corps of Southampton University.

By 1861 John Snook had moved to Bedford House, 77 Bedford Place, a noteworthy yellow brick house with a Doric portico, now "listed". Clearance has extinguished the former character of Amoy Street, whose frontages are now largely given over to car parking, but Canton Street still displays its original domestic architecture. Nicely combining variety of detail with consistency of scale, its groupings of neat small houses provide an attractive "period" townscape, now more highly esteemed than at any time since they were built some 130 years ago . . . for around £150 each!

Henry Joseph Buchan followed his father in business enterprise, Liberal politics and public service. He became a councillor in 1865, later an alderman, was elected mayor in 1871 and served as a J.P. for over twenty years. His support of local institutions and charities was complemented by the activities of his

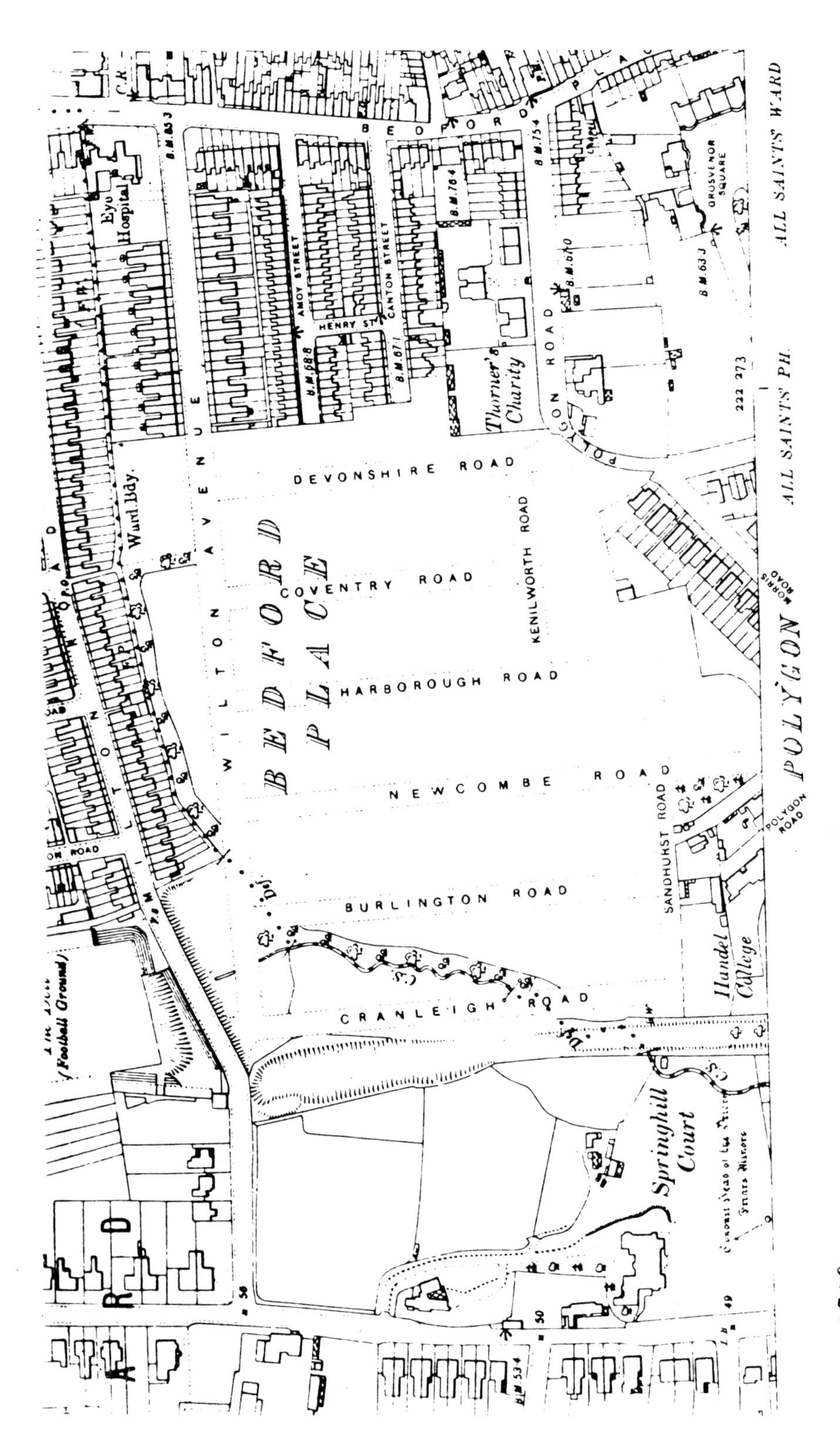
BEDFORD PLACE
POLYGON
ALL SAINTS' WARD
ALL SAINTS' PH.
WILTON AVENUE
DEVONSHIRE ROAD
COVENTRY ROAD
HARBOROUGH ROAD
NEWCOMBE ROAD
BURLINGTON ROAD
CRANLEIGH ROAD
KENILWORTH ROAD
SANDHURST ROAD
POLYGON ROAD
MORRIS ROAD
AMOY STREET
CANTON STREET
HENRY ST
GROSVENOR SQUARE
Eye Hospital
Ward Bdy.
Thorner's Charity
Handel College
Springhill Court
(Football Ground)
222 273
1910

H.J. Buchan as Mayor of Southampton in 1871 – oil painting by Frank Burcher (Courtesy Southampton Art Gallery, to which the portrait was presented in 1932 by his grand-daughter, Miss Alice Buchan).

Opposite: An excerpt from the O.S. map of 1910 showing new roads laid out on the Terrace House estate; the proposed Cranleigh Road was not developed.

wife Hannah (who died in 1885 at 72); she was responsible for establishing the "Mayoress's Blanket Loan Fund", continued for many years by her successors as "the means of doing incalculable good to many of the deserving poor of the town during the winter months".

H.J. Buchan extended the family business as "house decorator, glass factor etc." and became one of the town's largest employers, able to set an example to the building trades in 1871 by adopting the 9-hour day for his workmen. His most successful venture was the partnership he formed in 1848, joining his business acumen with the inventive genius of Captain George Peacock to produce anti-fouling compositions for ships' bottoms and preservative paints that were soon being exported world-wide in patent disposable containers. The firm of Peacock and Buchan established its steam-powered grinding and mixing works at Mousehole, later taking over the former mill and foundry there to develop its premises, now the Atlantic Works of Sealocrete Products Ltd.

George Peacock (1805-83), a man of wide-ranging experience as master mariner and engineer, came to Southampton in 1848, to serve the next ten years as docks master and superintendent. He had spent the previous eight years pioneering steam navigation along the west coast of South America. During the 1830s, when he was in the Royal Navy, he seized the opportunity to survey the Panama isthmus. Ferdinand de Lesseps later made generous acknowledgement of the value of his work as the basis for planning the canal. Peacock's later survey of the isthmus of Corinth also contributed to the construction of the canal there. His many inventions ranged from improvements in steam propulsion, screw propellors, chain and submarine telegraph cables and a widely adopted type of buoy to a combined life jacket and bathing costume "whereby both sexes may enjoy the pleasures of sea bathing with modesty and safety".

Peacock retired from his docks post in 1858 and found a new outlet for his energies as partner in a shipbroking firm, leaving the business at Southampton largely in the hands of Buchan. After the death of his widowed mother in 1876, H.J. Buchan moved into Wilton House and found a new interest, extending the greenhouses for growing choice orchids, which he often exhibited at the Southampton Horticultural Society's shows. This lively-minded Victorian "worthy", of "cheery and genial disposition", died on July 1, 1891, aged 77, with another claim to be remembered — he was the first Southampton man to request that his body be cremated.

Following Buchan's death, the sale of Wilton House led to further suburban development, involving the creation of Wilton Avenue and a new role for the late Georgian house whose name it was naturally given. The house still stands; it is surrounded by various later yellow brick extensions but above them can be seen the chimneys and parapet of the original white stucco building, with the faded lettering "Free Eye Hospital" across the top of it.

Captain George Peacock (1805-1883).

In 1894 Wilton House was bought by the committee established in 1890 to develop the eye hospital privately founded by Dr. John Follett Bullar. This enterprising and dedicated ophthalmic surgeon had opened his own eye clinic in 1889 in a rented house in Oxford Street: he soon leased another house and converted the two properties into a pioneer eye and ear hospital. A year later, this became a public institution, under a committee including Sir Thomas Longmore, of the Army Medical School at Netley, and his colleague, Surgeon General Maclean. With the latter as chairman and Rev. David Wauchope (after whom a ward was later named) as secretary, it energetically canvassed funds for larger premises.

Helped by donations of £1,000 each from two well-known local benefactors, Andrew Barlow and William Garton, it was enabled to purchase Wilton House for £3,072. Auctioning 80 ft. of building land along Wilton Avenue for £952 helped offset £2,531 spent on adaptations and fittings and the building was occupied in 1895. With the whole debt cleared by 1898, the "Free Eye Hospital" was firmly established, maintained by voluntary contributions and fund-raising efforts.

Amalgamation with the RSH Hospital was considered but a separate specialist eye hospital was thought best. Its original Ear, Nose and Throat department, conducted by Dr. J.A. Powell, was discontinued in 1899. Dr. Bullar served as honorary ophthalmic surgeon until 1912, when he was succeeded by Dr. Arthur Zorab, until his death in 1934. His son, Edward, afterwards served the hospital for 28 years until retirement in 1974. Miss M.A. Monk was the long-serving matron from 1894 to 1930.

Enjoying continuity and esteem, the hospital was enlarged and improved in 1907, 1924 and 1931. In 1923 the foundation stone for a £7,569 block of new wards was laid by Dr. Bullar. The founder, who retired to Guernsey, met his death in 1929, when he and his wife were victims of an air crash in the south of France. Although part of the National Health Service since 1948, the eye hospital he began in 1889 still retains its identity. Its facilities are becoming increasingly out-dated, however, and it awaits the Health Authority's decisions on funding and siting of modern replacement buildings.

Ahead of Wilton Avenue and Archers Road, the area between them that perpetuates the name Fitzhugh was developed for housing in the 1880s. One can now only speculate about the historical or political motivation for Cromwell and Milton being taken as road names there or whether Berkeley and Stanley Roads were intended as "aristocratic" complements to their republican associations. Stanley doubtless echoed the family name of the Earls of Derby — the 14th (1799-1869) was thrice Prime Minister for periods between 1852 and 1868: his eldest son (1826-93) served in the cabinets of both Disraeli and

The top of the original Wilton House can be seen above the later yellow brick frontage of the Free Eye Hospital. (Photograph: Tom Holder).

Gladstone. Elsewhere, Southampton has its Derby Road, named for either or both of them about 1875, and Stanley Road, St. Denys, originated a decade later. This duplication evidently caused confusion, resolved in 1900 when the Corporation redesignated its Fitzhugh counterpart as Holt Road. Why "Holt" was chosen is now unknown but there is nothing obscure about the naming of nearby Burton Road.

Along with sections of Milton Road styled Burton Place, Terrace and View, it was a parochial compliment to Rev. Arthur Daniel Burton, vicar of Shirley in 1884-89, who was active in seeking to meet the educational and religious needs of the rapidly growing population in the southern part of his parish. The original Fitzhugh National School off Burton Road was built in 1884 on a site given by Sir Edward Hulse (of Breamore House), who was then breaking up his Banister Court estate into building plots along Archers Road. The inscription above the school entrance records his gift and the fact that the school was erected at the expense of Andrew Barlow. The same benefactor (who lived at "Oatlands" in Winchester Road) provided an infants' school extension in 1887.

The school did double duty for worship while Mr. Burton — who had already established a mission church at Four Posts — sought funds to build a permanent church. He left Shirley in 1889 for Westmorland, where he served until retirement in 1922, and his pioneering work was continued by his successor, Rev. T.W.H. Jacob, and Rev. E.L. Franklin. The latter was curate for the St. Mark's district from 1887 and its first vicar from 1891 to 1917. Mr. Burton revisited Southampton to attend the consecration of St. Mark's by the Bishop of Guildford on December 8, 1891. The church cost some £6,500 — mostly given by Andrew Barlow and A.J. Day, of Northlands House, with Sir Edward Hulse again donating the site.

Recent years have seen significant changes around Burton Road. In 1968 what is now St. Mark's Middle School transferred to the former Western District school buildings off Shirley Road and the old school in Burton Road became a centre for special education. The lofty Victorian fabric of the church deteriorated to the point where repairs were impracticable and it was demolished in 1983. Proceeds from the sale of the site for new houses were applied to modernising and adapting the adjoining church hall (built in 1933) as a dual purpose centre for services and parish functions. What Mr. Burton would have thought of this "translation" of St. Mark's one cannot know — but at least his name remains firmly on the local street scene, along with others exemplifying many changes over the years in and around the Polygon area.

St. Mark's church, consecrated 1891, demolished 1983, from a postcard issued by Bealing and Hickson, c.1910.

André House, 1883, in Ordnance Road (Photograph: Tom Holder). Below: an enlargement of the photograph of the arch above the doorway.

The Changing Scene at Bellevue

Bellevue followed Bevois Mount as the most notable of the country mansions that encircled Southampton in the 18th and early 19th centuries, set in spacious grounds which became residential suburbs as the town expanded in Victorian times. The Bellevue estate was created from about 1766, occupying the 12 acre triangle stretching northwards from Brunswick Place, between London Road/ College Place and Bellevue Terrace/St. Mary's Road/Dorset Street.

James Linden's *Southampton Guide* of 1768 called Bellevue "superlatively the finest" of the "many excellent houses" along the road out of the town — "The whole is designed in the grandest style and, when finished, will form a superb pile. Nothing could be better situated than this spot, where Nature seems to aid the elegant taste of the accomplished owner".

The writer enthused over the "very grand prospect" from Bellevue (his turgid description was still being copied in local guidebooks fifty years later) but was forced to conclude "he can but faintly express his ideas of this noble structure and the various beauties it commands; he therefore wishes that every lover of the fine arts would visit this elegant seat and supply the defects of what he reads here by a personal survey".

Other contemporary accounts were lavish in praise of the green and hot houses — "scarcely to be equalled" — and the "excellent order" of the gardens, "replenished with every curious plant, shrub and flower that the enquiring mind and indefatigable curiosity of the ingenious owner could procure".

Baker's guide of 1804 noted "the back front, which alone we see from the (London) road, has nothing particular about it; the beauties of this very agreeable spot are best seen from the field called Marlands, where we have a full view of the south front, as well as of the noble greenhouse".

The mansion itself stood at the apex of the Bellevue site, north of Ordnance Road — which was laid out in 1883 in the penultimate phase of building over its grounds, followed by demolition of the old house in 1886. In Ordnance Road there is an attractive Victorian house with a stone tablet identifying it as "André House, 1883". Among the first houses built there, it was probably occupied by George Boyling, the builder responsible for most of the houses in Ordnance Road — where the leases specified minimum expenditure of £300-£350 each, to ensure good quality development as homes suitable for officers, engineers, pursers, ship brokers, merchants, accountants and, of course, Ordnance Survey staff.

Only the name of André House now recalls the creator and designer of Bellevue. Rightly described in 19th century guides as "that celebrated character", he was Nathaniel St. André (1680-1776). His creation of the house and layout of the grounds was a remarkable venture for a man well advanced in his eighties. He evidently had confidence in his future but although he lived on to 96 years, he never saw the mansion finished as he planned it.

Mr. Christie's particulars for the auction of Bellevue in 1776 waxed eloquent about the "spacious regular edifice, both the elevations adorned in a noble style of architecture; grand flights of steps rise magnificently to each entrance; the interior parts open with éclat; the decorations of the finished apartments display the elegance of the intended design and the number, size and arrangement of those unfinished demonstrate the utility of the plan, in which neatness, strength and excellence of materials are conspicuous". The purchaser was required to take "at a fair appraisement" all the building materials "now lying on the premises". It is doubtful if any later owner tried to complete the house and at some time early in the 19th century its original long facade was reduced by demolition of the unfinished wings.

What of the creator of Bellevue? Nathaniel St. André was born in Switzerland, and came to England as a boy servant with a rich family. Having the advantages of fluent French and German combined with musical ability and skill in dancing and fencing, he soon established himself in London, initially as a teacher. He then trained as a surgeon and anatomist and quickly developed a fashionable practice that brought him to the notice of George I, to whom command of German must have been an additional recommendation. St. André was appointed anatomist to the royal household in 1723 but his position at court effectively ended late in 1726, when he was unhappily involved in the curious case of Mary Toft, the "Rabbit Woman of Godalming".

The interest aroused by her extraordinary claims to have given birth to a succession of some fifteen rabbits extended to the court and led to St. André being sent to investigate them, along with Samuel Molyneux, a man of scientific repute, then secretary to the Prince of Wales. Somehow, St. André was completely deceived by Mary Toft. He published a credulous account of her supposed rabbit births. When her crude impositions were soon afterwards exposed by the celebrated obstetrician Sir Richard Manningham, who obtained her confession of these frauds, the gullible St. André was ridiculed and discredited, and made the butt of cartoons and squibs by Hogarth and others; pamphlets were even issued bound in rabbit skin.

Having already lost his position at court, St. André further compromised himself in 1728, when the former Lady Elizabeth Capel left with him immediately after her husband, Samuel Molyneux, collapsed and died in the House of Commons. St. André had treated him professionally and there were even suggestions that he had hastened Molyneux's death. Two years later, St. André married Lady Elizabeth (eldest daughter of the second Earl of Essex, with a substantial fortune of her own), but the scandal obliged them to leave London. The Earl of Peterborough was among the patients of St. André, who

This anonymous painting almost certainly portrays Nathaniel St. André in his later years at Southampton (Courtesy Southampton Art Gallery).

also treated Alexander Pope. Friendship with them probably influenced his coming to Southampton. Perhaps St. André had visited Peterborough's country mansion at Bevois Mount, which he later set out to emulate at Bellevue.

Holy Rood parish rate books show St. André established from 1742 at the handsome Georgian "town house" in the High Street, north of the Dolphin Hotel, into which it was later incorporated.

His earlier notoriety may not have initially followed him to Southampton, for the rate collector listed him until 1747 as "Mr. St. Andrew" before recognising "Nathaniel St. André esquire".

He bought the freehold of both house and hotel, leasing the latter to a succession of landlords but retaining occupation of 34 High Street until his death. He had it substantially improved and enlarged on a quadrangular pattern. St. André may also have been responsible in the 1760s for extending and remodelling the 'Dolphin' (which dated back to Tudor times) as a major coaching inn, with its elegant bay-windowed Assembly Room as the social centre of the town, then entering its heyday as a fashionable spa resort. St. André did not himself take any prominent part in its social activities or in municipal affairs. The only references to him in the Corporation journals concern his lease in 1762-69 of a ruined tower for a stable erected opposite the back gate of the 'Dolphin'.

He flourished in lively old age, retaining all his faculties and troubled only by gout. He is said to have considered women as "the prolongers of life". A close friend of his last twenty years, writing a sympathetic memoir of him in 1781 under the pseudonym "Impartial", noted that he was "all his life too much addicted to amours" — sometimes with those of lesser social standing. Besides enjoying the respect of a circle of friends who appreciated his entertaining conversation and skill at chess (and who carefully excluded rabbit from their dinner menus!), St. André was esteemed in Southampton for his "many acts of charity, kindness and benevolence to persons of every denomination" — as the *Hampshire Chronicle* wrote when recording his death on March 9, 1776 and burial in St. Mary's churchyard a week later.

The previous May he had enlarged his estate by purchasing Banister Court farmhouse and 136 acres; at this time his only recognition of advancing years was granting a long lease on his London house, in George Street, Hanover Square. All St. André's Southampton properties — High Street house, Dolphin Hotel, Banister and Bellevue estates, together with 21 adjoining acres "called East Marlens, otherwise Maudlins" — were auctioned at Bellevue by Mr. Christie on July 29, 1776.

St. André's will provided for most of the proceeds to be applied for the benefit of William Henry and George Frederick Pitt, the sons of Mary Pitt, "my late servant". George was born in 1766, William a few years earlier. Brought up as gentlemen by St. André's trustees, both seem to have made their careers as army officers. William died in 1824 and it was through his brother that Southampton Corporation received in 1831 what is known as the "Pitt Collection" of rare books.

Before showing himself absurdly credulous in the Mary Toft affair, St. André enjoyed repute in medical circles, as surgeon of Westminster Hospital and the first anatomist to give public lectures in London, using his own improved models. He learnt his medicine and surgery by apprenticeship and study, building up a library of over 700 books — acquired by the Royal College of Surgeons in 1818 at the bargain price of £152. These were part of the library of 3,593 items which St. André left in trust for the Pitt brothers in 1776. It included many books originally belonging to his wife's first husband, Samuel Molyneux (1689-1728) and his father William Molyneux (1656-98), both Fellows of the Royal Society with wide scientific and other interests. St. André carefully augmented their collection.

In 1831 G.F. Pitt, then living at Millbrook, gave the surviving 1,100 volumes to Southampton Corporation "in order to encourage the pursuit of literature and general information among the inhabitants of this town". They were kept in the Audit House. Their specialised content did not suit use as a public reference library, and in 1862 the Pitt collection was transferred to the newly established Hartley Institution. Thirty years later the collection was returned to Southampton Public Library, which still holds it. A full catalogue was published in 1964 to mark the visit to Southampton of the British Association.

The ownership and occupation of Bellevue following the 1776 auction sale is unclear but from 1786 it was the residence of Rear Admiral Sir Richard King (1730-1806). Born at Gosport, he entered the navy as a boy and served in various expeditions and engagements, steadily rising in commands. One capture of a rich Spanish galleon off Manila brought him personal prize money of over £30,000. Admiral's rank and a knighthood were his rewards for gallantry in action against the French in 1782.

While at Bellevue, he became a "serving burgess" of Southampton and made his contribution to municipal affairs, as well as on the social scene. He was still listed in 1793 as a member of the Royal Southampton Archers, but from 1790 he was commanding fleets in the Downs and at Spithead. His Southampton connection must have ended in 1792 when he was created a baronet and appointed governor and Commander-in-Chief at Newfoundland; two years later he became C.-in-C. at Plymouth.

His only son, another Sir Richard King (1774-1834), also followed a naval career and became an admiral — as did his own son.

A

PARTICULAR

AND

CONDITIONS of SALE

OF THE

Freehold, Copyhold and Leafehold Eftates

OF

Nathaniel St. Andre, Efq;

DECEASED,

SITUATE

In and near the TOWN of *SOUTHAMPTON*;

WHICH WILL BE SOLD BY AUCTION,

(By ORDER of the EXECUTORS)

By Mr. CHRISTIE,

At Lot I. Belle Vüe, near *Southampton* aforefaid,

On MONDAY, JULY 29, 1776, at Eleven o'Clock.

A Perfon attends on the Premifes (Lot I. and IV.) to fhew the fame.

Bellevue House – front view, from an early 19th century painting.

Opposite: Front page of Mr. Christie's "particular" for the auction at Bellevue in 1776 (Courtesy Southampton Record Office).

In 1903, the Borough Council ended duplication of the name of Park Road (laid out around 1850 across the southern part of Bellevue grounds or park) by changing it to the more distinctive King's Park Road. It may have had in mind Sir Richard King rather than — or as well as — the reigning monarch. Whatever the intention, the name serves to recall the admiral in the context of Bellevue nearly two centuries ago.

Southampton guidebooks of 1793-1800 noted Bellevue as owned by a Mr. Chambers, then a minor, but by 1802 it became the "seat" of Josias Jackson, a retired West Indian planter with extensive estates in St. Vincent. Doubtless winning friends by his lavish hospitality, he became prominent in local affairs, notably as colonel of the militia corps of 1803, the Loyal Southampton Fusiliers. In June, 1804, Mrs. Jackson presented them with new colours and marked the occasion by entertaining "a numerous company of fashionables" at Bellevue.

In 1806, Jackson came to the fore as leader of a group of property owners in the neighbourhood of The Avenue who opposed the decision of the Corporation to fell every alternate one of the trees planted sixty years earlier across the Common. The tree felling was at the request of the Southampton and Winchester Turnpike Trust, which wanted more light and air admitted to its road.

Jackson's group secured an injunction to restrain the Corporation from reducing the amenities to which all the town's inhabitants were entitled. However, the Corporation got the Lord Chancellor to over-rule this decision, on the grounds that the Corporation could do as it liked with its own trees.

Jackson was encouraged to stand for election as one of two Southampton M.P.s in 1806 but he came third and last in the poll. There was another general election in 1807, when he was returned unopposed. In 1812 he first offered himself for re-election but then made a last-minute withdrawal and shortly afterwards left Southampton.

He was followed at Bellevue by Admiral Sir Richard Rodney Bligh (1737-1821), who came of the same old Cornish naval family as his contemporary William Bligh, of breadfruit and *Bounty* fame, although their relationship was distant.

Sir Richard held various commands during his long naval career and was a veteran of numerous actions. His most celebrated exploit was aboard HMS *Alexander* in 1794, engaging single-handed a whole French squadron of nine warships. Several hours of fighting resulted in the French suffering ten times as many casualties as the *Alexander*, which inflicted great damage on her opponents before being obliged to strike her colours, in an almost sinking condition. Her commander spent a year in a French prison before being returned to England and afterwards serving in the West Indies.

Admiral Sir Richard Rodney Bligh, from a painting by John Opie. (Courtesy Southampton City Museums).

Sir Richard Bligh has his family name perpetuated by the roads deriving from "Blighmont", the house he had built for his son Captain George Miller Bligh — after his recovery from severe wounds received at Trafalgar, where he served as Nelson's flag lieutenant on the *Victory*.

The name "Blighmont" was a semi-French creation of the style then fashionable, combining the owner's name with an indication of the comparatively elevated position of the house at Millbrook (to the north-east of the modern British-American Tobacco factory), standing in an estate of about fifty acres west of Waterhouse Lane.

Blighmont, about 1941 (Courtesy Southampton Central Library).

Captain Bligh left Blighmont about 1835, after which the eight-bedroom house passed through various ownerships, with its grounds gradually reduced by Victorian and later housing developments. Blighmont Crescent and Blighmont Avenue were built in 1920-24. The remainder of the estate was bought by the British-American Tobacco Company as the site for its factory, opened in 1926. Blighmont House was run as a nursing home for over forty years, until demolished in 1963.

Lady Bligh, the admiral's widow, lived on at Bellevue until 1835. Two years later, the estate was bought by John Drew (1767-1841). He was then living at Sussex Place, Above Bar, in one of the fashionable terrace houses he had

A different sort of elegance – Blighmont Crescent soon after the houses were built in 1922 (from a postcard issued by George Ayles, of Testwood Road Post Office).

earlier built — and named in compliment to the Duke of Sussex, sixth son of George III. Drew removed to Bellevue some time before census night in 1841 but did not long enjoy his new home, for he died the same year.

John Drew claimed descent from the Comtes de Dreux (in Brittany) and back to Hugh Capet, crowned King of France in 987. Centuries later, one of the family, adhering to the Huguenot faith, was obliged to leave France to avoid religious persecution after 1685. He settled as a trader in Portsmouth, whence his son, another John Drew (the English version of Jean de Dreux), moved to Southampton about 1710 and set up as a brewer at the corner of Houndwell Lane/Above Bar. A family business prospered, transferring to larger premises on the site of the later Queen's Buildings.

The John Drew who bought Bellevue was born at Portsea, married a Miss Watkins while holding an excise post in Kent, and came to Southampton in 1796 to join his uncle, a Mr. Heather, who had a gin distillery in French Street. There John Drew took over the "Fish and Kettle"; he later bought the premises 100 High Street, where he built his own malt house and brewery, followed in 1816 by the addition of No. 99 and the erection of a range of buildings and house in Broad Lane. From these, John Drew's business interests expanded to the extent that he left property amounting to one fortieth of the whole Southampton rating assessment. On the basis of this inheritance, his son John Watkins Drew (1795-1892) — who had earlier joined his father in partnership — retired from the brewing business in 1842.

Earlier, he had campaigned for the 1832 Reform Bill, helped establish the Liberal weekly *Hampshire Independent* and been actively involved from their outset as a director of the companies promoting the railway, docks and floating bridge. After 1842 he had the means and leisure to enjoy extensive foreign travels, hunt with the New Forest hounds and sail his yacht in the Solent. Drew did not long remain in Bellevue, which around 1845 he briefly leased to the Marquis of Conyngham. He himself returned to live at Sussex Place. From about 1850 he made the southern part of the Bellevue estate available on 1,000 year building leases, laying out (King's) Park Road, Dorset Street and Bellevue Road.

By 1830, the estate name had been adopted for a row of fashionable houses at Bellevue Place, on the west side of London Road opposite St. Paul's church. The comparable Bellevue Terrace was developed along the north-eastern edge of Bellevue grounds from the 1840s. Incongruously, Bellevue Street, built to the south-east by 1830, had no pretensions to gentility, being one of the hastily erected rows of poor dwellings at Charlotte Place that became a hotbed of cholera in 1849. Its existence ended in 1967, when it was absorbed into a car park.

Drew's development of the Bellevue grounds from 1850 gave Andrew Lamb, P. and O. superintendent engineer at Southampton, the opportunity to acquire land in the south-east corner, on which he had St. Andrew's Villa built off Brunswick Place; he donated the adjoining site for St. Andrew's Presbyterian Church, built in 1852-53.

In October, 1853 J.W. Drew leased Bellevue House and its remaining grounds north of Bellevue Road to Rev. James Duncan, who transferred there in 1854 his Southampton Collegiate School — which he had opened ten years previously, as the Diocesan School, in Prospect Place. It had the patronage of the Bishop of Winchester and other diocesan clergy and its prospectus stated "the object of this institution is to combine the advantages of a solid and varied education with the most liberal and gentlemanly treatment. The terms are calculated in the lowest scale that can consist with the attainment of these advantages". They were 40/45 guineas a year for boys under/over 12 as boarders and 12 guineas for day pupils — to include "the whole course of education, except German and Music", which were extras.

"The course of study is directed to preparation for the Universities, Naval

Philip Brannon's engraving of the Diocesan Collegiate School at Prospect Place, 1850.

and Military Colleges, Commissions in the Army, direct appointments to the East India Company's service, and for Professional pursuits in general." The school evidently met a need at the time as the old Grammar School was in decline (and indeed was temporarily suspended in the 1850s). The success of Mr. Duncan's school made necessary the move to larger premises at Bellevue, offering playing fields and a gymnasium, the latter by conversion of the former orangery and potting shed. By 1860 it was styled the Southampton College and Boarding School, its status enhanced by addition of the Bishops of Bengal, Madras and Bombay to the list of patrons, while its object was redefined as "to ensure to the sons of Noblemen and Gentlemen a high Collegiate Education, with the care and comfort of a first-class Boarding School".

The College was continued after Duncan's death for another ten years until 1886 by his widow, with Dr. D. Tierney as principal. In 1883 Mrs. M. Duncan took a new 7-year lease of Bellevue from Miss Kate M. Drew (J.W. Drew had by then made over most of his property to his daughter, who lived until 1926), with the grounds reduced by the laying out of Ordnance Road, where house building started that year. Three years later Mrs. Duncan decided to give up running the College. The old house and grounds were thereupon put up for auction, the former for its materials prior to demolition, the latter for building development along The Avenue — where the names College Place and Terrace were adopted to recall the final phase of Bellevue's history.

In 1927 the Council agreed to a request from the occupiers for College Place and Terrace, along with Avenue Place, to be combined and re-numbered under the name of College Place.

Asylum Green, the grassy strip extending northwards up the centre of The Avenue, carries in its name a reminder of the institution which a century and a half ago occupied the buildings taken over in 1841 by the Ordnance Survey. Although at one time mainly associated with lunatics, an asylum is more widely defined as any place of shelter or refuge for those needing care and protection. From October, 1816 a branch of the Royal Military Asylum, established at Chelsea in 1803, was accommodated in the former "horse barracks" erected from 1794, which became redundant after war with France ended in 1815.

Over the years 1816-30, the then considerable sum of £15,956 was recorded as spent on adapting and enlarging them to house 400 boys — soldiers' sons who had lost one or both parents. With military precision, annual expenditure on their care and maintenance was then calculated at £8.2s.11½d per boy. For this, they seem to have been well clothed and fed. They received half a pint of beer a day with their dinner — which on Sundays included eight ounces of roast beef. With their bread and cheese suppers they were given half pints of beer or milk on alternate days. To begin the day, the boys were "caused to rise by beat of drum at 6 a.m. in summer and 7 a.m. in winter". For their welfare, resident staff included the commandant, surgeon, chaplain and

Bellevue, south elevation, about 1880, from a photograph by C.G. Ellaby (Courtesy Southampton City Museums).

superintendent of morals and education, with several sergeants "strictly charged to abstain from and to check all profane and improper language". There were nurses "to take care that the children shall be properly washed and combed and their clothes decently put on; and that their feet be regularly washed at night three times a week in summer and twice a week in winter".

The boys wore uniform comprising linen shirt, jacket of scarlet cloth, breeches, worsted stockings, stout shoes and a leather cap. They were "instructed in the principles of the established church, writing, elementary arithmetic, geography etc., also to knit and make their own shirts, jackets, trousers and shoes". Eventually, "when arrived at a proper age and thought fit, they are disposed of as apprentices or, with their own free consent, enter the regular army as private soldiers". In 1823 all the boys (except infants for whom a separate branch of the Asylum had earlier been set up at Parkhurst) were moved back to Chelsea and girls were brought to Southampton to take their place. Their instruction was limited to "the principles of the established church and useful domestic duties", preparatory to placing in "situations" which one contemporary called "domestic servitude".

The numbers of children "deemed objects of this charitable design" gradually diminished and late in 1840 the remaining girls were withdrawn back to Chelsea. The empty Asylum buildings were thus available to meet the emergency needs of the Ordnance Survey, which came to Southampton literally by accident, moving into them on November 12, 1841, a fortnight after fire had destroyed its original headquarters in the Tower of London.

The Ordnance Survey staff then comprised 31 military personnel and 83 civilians, sixty of them classified as "computers" — men who painstakingly undertook complicated trigonometrical calculations, without benefit of microchips. At first unenthusiastic about its enforced move, the Ordnance Survey establishment soon took root at its new base and identified itself with Southampton. As its staff and activities expanded, the old barracks and Asylum building were altered and replaced to suit its requirements. The surviving mid-Victorian blocks were designed in the 1860s by the Director General of the Ordnance Survey, General Sir Henry James, RE, KCB, FRS, who nicely harmonised them with the house in which he himself lived at the north-east corner of the site.

This solidly imposing three-storey yellow brick building of 1840 was one of the last projects of Samuel Edward Toomer (1801-42), the local architect responsible for Rockstone Place, an attractive Regency-style terrace comprising four groups of three houses, erected in 1833-41 in a secluded position on the northern fringe of what it helped to make "the genteel upper part" of the expanding town. Originally a private residence styled Avenue House, it was taken over about 1865 by the Ordnance Survey, to become "The Director General's House". Keeping this name, the recently restored "Grade II listed building" has since September, 1986 served a new role, as prestige offices for the stockbrokers Cobbold Roach and Co., an Anglo-Australian firm which incorporates the business started in Southampton in 1892 by Arthur Hills Cobbold.

Following severe bomb damage in 1940, the Ordnance Survey divided its activities between its London Road premises, others at Chessington in Surrey and the Crabwood House site at Maybush, until concentrated there in its new permanent headquarters, completed in 1969. The former OS site in London Road has recently been redeveloped by the building of new Law Courts, opened in 1987, on a plan which happily preserves the best of the "listed" Victorian buildings there.

On the southern tip of Asylum Green — preserved by being moved there, twenty yards north of its original position, during road works in 1966 — stands another mid-Victorian structure now accorded "listed building" status. Disused since 1939 and isolated in the midst of today's heavy traffic around it, but enduring for nearly a century and a quarter, this elaborate drinking fountain bears an inscription proclaiming it "the gift of Mr. Councillor John Ransom to his native town", in 1865.

Although the clearance and redevelopment of Ransom's Terrace (once part of Albert Road) removed his name from the street scene, Ransom's fountain remains a feature of the townscape, serving as a sort of self-created memorial to the colourful character who liked to boast — not without reason — of being Southampton's biggest shipowner. John Ransom (1799-1886) prospered as the owner of a score or more of small wooden vessels, most launched from his own yards or rebuilt there from salvaged wrecks. Some carried timber and other cargoes across the Atlantic, others traded to northern Europe and the Mediterranean, but most were engaged around British coasts, laden with coal and building materials. Ransom's business also included repair work for the P. and O. and Royal Mail lines and other shipping interests.

He was a typical Victorian "self-made man" who, to quote the *Hampshire Advertiser* obituary, "raised himself from small beginnings to a position of considerable opulence". Sir James Lemon testified that although Ransom had little education, "he possessed a great deal of shrewdness and business capacity".

His two brothers were market gardeners at Northam and Hill Lane but he was apprenticed to shipbuilding. By 1823 he was himself building wooden ships in association with James Blaker at the Chapel yard; six years later he was working with John Rubie at Cross House yard, where he afterwards took control. Ransom kept the 'White Swan" at Cross House, where his workmen had to call for their wages on Saturdays — doubtless more to the benefit of landlord-employer than wives waiting for house-keeping money!

Ransom took over the Belvidere yard from James Blaker in 1852, expanded it and later concentrated his activities there. One of the last ships built at Cross House in 1870 was the 103-ton schooner *Hannah Ransom* (named after his wife), which enjoyed a working career lasting until it was wrecked in 1919. Other Ransom-built ships earlier suffered similar fates, among them vessels named *Crosshouse, Belvidere, Lady Hulse* and *Lady Heathcote*. The latter two were named in compliment to the families whose Breamore and Hursley Park estates provided timber for them, as also the largest ships built at the Belvidere yard — the *Louisa Malcolm* (for Mrs. Malcolm of Beechwood), of 699 tons in 1872, and the *May Hulse*, 463 tons, launched in 1881 as one of Ransom's last.

When Ransom died in 1886, at the age of 87, his Belvidere yard was run down and dilapidated. He left the property and his ships to his nephew and yard manager, James Dible, who, with his sons, continued ship building, repairing and operating at Northam for another three decades. Dible's and Belvidere Wharfs memorialise the Ransom era along the Itchen.

From 1851 until his death, Ransom lived at Hawthorn Cottage, the attractive house built in 1814 on the site of the old brickworks at the south end of the Common. For many years, "Johnny" was a familiar sight, being driven in his carriage down to Northam or the Audit House in the High Street. He became a notable figure in the robust local politics of his day, holding as a Conservative a Council seat for the usually Liberal ward of St. Mary's from 1860 to 1868, after which he sat as an alderman for the next six years. Ransom was long remembered as a "card" — a colourful character noted for his pithy remarks and malapropisms. Exulting after the declaration of his first narrow victory at the polls in 1860, his triumphant cry at his defeated Liberal opponents "where be 'em now?" became a long-lasting catchphrase in the politics of Victorian Southampton. Ransom dispensed lavish hospitality to celebrate his election victories, likewise the inauguration of his drinking fountain on Asylum Green.

After the old Padwell Cross pond and animal pound (for cattle grazed on the Common) had been filled in and superseded — having become an insanitary nuisance by 1850 — Ransom "met the needs for a water supply for way-worn cattle and horses" and their thirsty masters by commissioning what contemporaries acclaimed "a chaste and elegant structure". Designed by the local architect-surveyor Josiah George Poole and carved by Sansom of London, the stone fountain incorporated columns, carved figures and drinking bowls on its four sides — with the injunction "drink but waste not" — under a domed top surmounted by a decorated cross; a drinking trough was placed alongside it.

After its official inauguration on November 2, 1865, Ransom "hospitably regaled" his Council colleagues and friends with a lavish banquet at his Horton's

The inauguration of John Ransom's drinking fountain on Asylum Green – November 2, 1865. The donor stands beside the fountain, at the left. (Courtesy Southampton City Museums).

Heath farm. He also acquired a farm at Bartley and took pride in breeding prize-winning pigs. Ransom became a substantial property owner, besides running a large timber business. His timber yard was at Ransom's Terrace (the section of the later Albert Road between Anglesea Terrace and Chantry Road), where he owned a row of 35 houses, built for his employees in the early 1850s, as one of the first developments in the area of the former town marsh. Other houses from which Ransom drew rents included 27 in Blackberry Terrace: their demolition recently revealed the old ships' timbers used in their construction.

Further up the Avenue beyond Ransom's fountain, there has stood since 1909 another piece of carved stonework also now designated a "Grade II building of special architectural or historical interest". Moved some forty yards north of its original position during road improvements in 1967, it now stands almost opposite Brighton Road, little noticed on the grassy strip dividing streams of traffic. Few pedestrians cross the carriageways to read the inscription repeated on each side of the centre section — "Presented to the Town of Southampton by a native and lifelong resident in commemoration of his 60th birthday, October 7, 1909". Carvings on the middle of the three urns surmounting this memorial depict Canute rebuking his courtiers and the departure of the *Mayflower*. They are good examples of the stonemason's art, for the donor of this anonymous "building" was John Daniel Haysom.

Haysom was at that time engaged with others, notably Professor F.J.C. Hearnshaw, of Hartley University College, in promoting and raising funds for a major memorial to the *Mayflower*; it was erected by the family firm of Garret and Haysom in 1913. J.D. Haysom himself did not live to see its unveiling, for he died on November 24, 1911, aged 62, at his home in Brighton Road. He had been a principal of the firm of monumental masons responsible over many decades for numerous public monuments and cemetery memorials, mural tablets and other carved stonework, in Southampton and elsewhere.

The City Record Office holds its extensive business archive, dating back almost to its foundation in 1806 by John Garret, a bricklayer from Portsea. His son, George, bought property in East Street around 1822 and developed the business that became J. and H. Garret, "architectural stone carvers and masons".

Martyn Haysom was working separately as a stonemason in Trinity Road during the middle years of the 19th century, followed by his son, John, until Garret and Haysom joined in partnership about 1877. Their "memorial, tomb and gravestone works" at 105-106 East Street was rebuilt and enlarged as the "Eastgate Monumental and Ecclesiastical Masonry Works" in 1899. A year later, the firm was honoured by a royal warrant of appointment as "statuary masons" to Queen Victoria, recognising work done at Osborne, Carisbrooke and Whippingham church.

Hawthorn Cottage, erected on Southampton Common about 1815.
(Courtesy Southampton Record Office).

Beyond his craft, J.D. Haysom devoted himself in many ways to serving his town, particularly in its historical, educational and cultural activities. He may now be forgotten but his anonymous memorial endures as part of the Southampton townscape.

Quite separate from Asylum Green in the origin of its name is Asylum Road, off Bellevue Road. Really only a back lane, it does not seem to have found its way into the street directory until about 1950, to provide an address for businesses established there, but the name was in local use much earlier — as Asylum Lane, which from 1853 gave rear access to the Hampshire Female Orphan Asylum fronting Park Road (re-named King's Park Road in 1903).

This charitable institution was founded on September 24, 1837, by Dr. and Mrs. Lindoe, to care for some of the many unwanted or orphan children of that time. Initially catering for six girls in a house at Kingsland Place, it transferred in 1840 to premises in Albion Place, where four times as many could be accommodated. Guidebooks of the 1840s noted it as "a small asylum for female orphans, well supported and superintended by benevolent ladies". They included familiar names like Miss Bullar (Doctors Joseph and William Bullar were the Asylum's medical attendants); Miss Chamberlayne; Mrs. Fanshawe, wife of the vicar of Holy Trinity, North Front, later Rector of All Saints; and Mrs. Jellicoe, whose husband Samuel Jellicoe was treasurer of the Asylum, with which the Jellicoe family long maintained a close supporting connection.

The famous Admiral of World War I has made the Jellicoe name celebrated. Those of Fanshawe and Bullar are little remembered. Fanshawe and Bullar Streets in Newtown, laid out from 1844 around the Royal South Hants Infirmary, are unusual among Southampton street names: they accorded commemoration during their lifetimes to the prime movers in establishing that long-lasting institution, which had that year moved into its new buildings sited on what was then the edge of the town.

Rev. Charles Simon Faithfull Fanshawe was vicar of Holy Trinity from 1837 to 1846, then rector of All Saints until 1855. For these eighteen years he was energetically involved in promoting the spiritual and material welfare of his parishioners and other inhabitants, particularly in matters of public health and elementary education. He was responsible for organising the efforts leading to the opening of "National" schools for the children of both his parishes — Holy Trinity in 1839 and All Saints in 1848.

In helping to establish the R.S.H. Infirmary, he supported a project growing out of the small casualty ward which Joseph Bullar had taken the initiative in opening in a house at South Front, Kingsland, in 1838, following the disastrous fire at a High Street warehouse the previous November — whose 22 victims are memorialised on the tablets still to be seen on the front of Holyrood church. Joseph Bullar and his brother, William, maintained a busy general practice at Prospect Place for many years until their deaths in 1869 and also gave much of their time and skill as surgeons at the R.S.H., of which they were the mainstays; Joseph was its creative genius, William its dedicated secretary. They applied a testimonial fund in 1856 to financing a new west wing of the hospital, comprising the upper and lower Bullar wards, as a memorial to their sister, Anne. How a road at Bitterne Park was later named in honour of their father, the schoolmaster John Bullar, has been told in *Streets*, pages 83-84.

The early Victorian promoters of the Female Orphan Asylum combined benevolence, morality and practical charity — "the design of this institution is to rescue destitute children from the contaminating examples of Idleness and Vice: and by instilling into their minds the principles of Religion and Morality, accustoming them to habits of constant industry and cheerful obedience, and instructing and employing them in every kind of household work, to qualify them for service in respectable families". By the end of 1853, the Asylum had received 66 girls, of whom 27 had been placed out "in service", eight removed by friends, with 31 then remaining in its care.

The 1853 report, the earliest preserved in the City Record Office, gave the year's expenditure as precisely £482.9s.6d., which was all covered by subscriptions, donations and collections. Patrons were the Bishop and Archdeacon of Winchester, supported by various titled "patronesses".

By 1853 the Asylum had moved to its new premises — one of the first buildings on the Bellevue "park" (between Brunswick Place and Bellevue Road) which John Watkins Drew was then making available for residential development. At the end of the year only £81 was needed to cover the cost of the new building, exclusive of £370 for the site. The new Asylum was opened for public inspection every Thursday afternoon. Its committee was anxious that subscribers should visit it "in order to be satisfied as to the manner in which the funds have been expended: every measure has been adopted that prudence and economy could sanction".

The status of the charity was later enhanced by the patronage of "His Serene Highness the Prince Edward of Saxe-Weimar", which may have helped it gather funds to build a £2,000 extension in 1887. Later additions enabled the Hampshire Girls Orphanage (as it was re-named) to cater for 90 girls in the 1930s, at a cost of some £2,000 a year, all raised by voluntary endeavour. Sir Russell Bencraft (see *Streets*, pages 47-49) was its energetic president and chairman for over twenty years between the wars.

After the war and changed social and political circumstances ended its activities as a private charity, the buildings in King's Park Road were used as a Council health clinic, until this transferred in 1962 to the new central clinic at East Park Terrace. The premises then served other Corporation purposes and accommodated the Citizens' Advice Bureau and Marriage Guidance Council from 1968 to 1977. They were demolished and replaced by purpose-built offices for these two voluntary organisations, which moved back to King's Park Road in 1981, as tenants of the City Council.

The site thus spans fourteen decades of use for various forms of community service, exemplified by the name of Asylum Road.

Brunswick Place was named in compliment to Caroline of Brunswick, following her ill-fated marriage in 1795 to her cousin, the Prince of Wales — afterwards Prince Regent and later George IV. In Georgian and Regency times, streets were often given royal or aristocratic names, not only as expressions of patriotism, loyalty or respect but also, one suspects, because developers hoped that such associations, albeit only nominal, would provide a "good address" to enhance the tone of their "spec built" terraces. Topographically, however, Brunswick Place has a much longer and more complex history than its name suggests, for it was the outcome of an impoverished widow's charitable bequest made many years before the land was built upon.

Making her will in 1665, Katherine Wulfris must have looked back sadly on domestic difficulties when she wrote "I give unto my son John Wulfris of London, merchant — by whom I and my executrix (her daughter, another Katherine) have lost the greatest part of the estate — the sum of five shillings, to bar him from any right or title to any part of my estate that I shall leave behind me". However reduced this may have been, it still included an orchard, then let to George Head for £2 a year, which she bequeathed to the churchwardens of her native parish of Holyrood, "for clothing and placing out of one poor maid to some apprenticeship or service".

A century later, this field, known as Giddy Bridge, was let to Nathaniel St. André as part of his Bellevue "pleasure grounds". In 1770, he paid £5 a year for it. In 1792, on the departure of the then owner of Bellevue, Admiral Sir Richard King, who had paid five times as much to lease this addition to his "park", the Holyrood churchwardens sought further to increase their income from the land.

The Wulfris bequest gave them the benefit of all future improvements on the former orchard, for which they offered a 99-year lease by public auction on June 25, 1792. The highest bid was £51 a year from John Simpkins: after a Chancery suit (costing £192, which had to be met from the rent), the Holyrood trustees were empowered to grant him a lease from 1795. Unlike John Simpson, the London speculator who that same year began laying out Albion Place off the High Street, Simpkins was a local man of business who likewise had an eye for land "ripe for development" with "genteel residences". Leases and deeds variously described him as upholsterer, auctioneer and inn-holder. He was listed at the "Coach and Horses" in Above Bar by the town directory of 1803 but not in the 1811 edition, by which time he had retired to be "now of Hill in the parish of Millbrook, gentleman". Simpkins died at his home there — Spring Place, in 1815, aged 69.

The "piece of garden" he had secured measured some 145-165 yards from east to west, tapering in depth from 43 yards on the east to 15 yards on the west. It bordered on East Marlands common field, held by John Fox, from whom in 1796 Simpkins negotiated the lease of a strip of land 426 ft. long and 23-25 ft. wide. This enabled him to form a road in front of the house plots into which he divided his holding. Over the next fifteen years he disposed of them on building leases for the remainder of his 99-year term.

To secure uniformity and select residential character, the deeds (copies of which are preserved in the City Record Office) required a "good and substantial messuage or tenement" — then costing about £500 — to be built within two years "according to the elevation designed for all the allotments" and "as nearly as possible the materials and symmetry perfectly to correspond". Stringent prohibitions were imposed on using the properties for offensive trades or causing any "nuisance" to other tenants.

Brunswick Place as it was before re-development (Courtesy Southampton Central Library).

Associated with Simpkins was the architect John Plaw (1745-1820), who had made his name in London before moving to Southampton about 1794. He is remembered for three popular "pattern books" of "rural architecture" which went through several editions between 1785 and 1813. His best known buildings were the romantic circular house on an island in Lake Windermere (1775) and a quaintly "geometrical" church at Paddington, consecrated in 1791 and later noteworthy for its memorial to the great actress Sarah Siddons, buried there in 1831.

In Southampton, Plaw was probably responsible for designing the original cavalry barracks in London Road. He was involved in planning the fashionable terraces at Albion Place as well as Brunswick Place but neither of these ambitious schemes were fully realised. A town map of 1802 showed Brunswick Place laid out, with a house at each end, but "the circumstances of the time" —

wars with France — deterred speculative building in an area still regarded as distantly suburban. Delays in development may have influenced "John Plaw, Spring Place, Hill, architect" to quit the Southampton scene in 1809 and settle in Canada.

With the return of peace in 1815, building revived and in 1824 the Charity Commissioners noted that the Wulfris site was fully occupied with eleven "well built houses, stated to be worth £50-£100 each per annum". For poor rates, they were then valued at £20-£25 each, with one at £37 and the largest at £60. This was "Brunswick House", which still adorns the townscape with its neat stucco frontage, Tuscan portico and cast iron railings — now the only survivor of the original buildings in Brunswick Place. It was fitted in at the narrow

Brunswick House, at the west end of Brunswick Place, is the only original building surviving there from the early 19th century. (Photograph: Tom Holder).

The Park House, a late Victorian office building, on the site of the former garden of Brunswick House. (Photograph: Tom Holder).

west end of the Wulfris land, with a large garden alongside it; this was used in 1894 for the attractive late Victorian "Park House", which adds variety to the street scene.

Formerly known as Vectis Terrace, this group of five yellow brick bow-windowed houses was added to Brunswick Place in the 1850s. (Photograph: Tom Holder).

Further east, there survives an elegant group of five 3-storey houses in warm yellow brick, with large first floor bow windows. Known as Vectis Terrace until 1900, this dates from the 1850s, as an eastward extension of old Brunswick Place, incorporating part of the Bellevue grounds.

Meanwhile, under a scheme adopted in 1803, the Holyrood churchwardens were annually apprenticing six children (usually boys rather than "maids") at £8 each, with a seventh grant made every fifth year. After the properties reverted to them on expiry of the lease in 1894, the Wulfris trustees applied for a new scheme of management for their enhanced income. Their houses and sites in Brunswick Place, let at £20 to £90 a year, then brought in £655, with another £25 from rents on Nos. 2, 4 and 6 London Road, leased for 99 years from 1894.

In 1899, the Charity Commissioners authorised the trustees (now including representatives of the local authorities and Hartley College) to spend up to £150 on "apprenticing to some useful trade or occupation meritorious children (boys and girls equally) resident in the borough of Southampton" and to make grants to institutions "offering special advantages to apprentices", also non-denominational orphanages. A third of the available balance was earmarked for scholarships of £10-£15 a year over 2-4 years to boys attending grammar schools and Hartley College. The remaining two-thirds was set aside to accumulate until 1906, when a further scheme authorised its application "for the secondary education of poor girls".

The annual statement of the Wulfris Foundation for 1919-20 showed £644 income, with £371 paid to beneficiaries and the rest spent mainly on property maintenance. Since then, money values have greatly changed and genteel residences have given way to modern offices in post-war Brunswick Place. The Wulfris trustees have disposed of their properties there and now administer the greatly increased income from their resulting capital investments. In changed social and economic conditions, what is now the Wulfris Educational Foundation has itself changed with them, to meet wider needs more flexibly.

In 1932 boys' scholarships were extended to cover fees and maintenance allowances for university students. Distinctions between the sexes ended in 1961, when the current "Wulfris" scheme was approved by the Ministry of Education. The trustees now apply the Foundation's income "for the benefit of persons of either sex, resident in Southampton, who have not attained the age of 25 years". Grants may include scholarships and allowances at schools, universities or other places of learning; assistance in connection with "a profession, trade or calling"; travel to pursue studies abroad; provision for physical training and coaching; and help to study "music or other arts".

So the orchard bequeathed by Katherine Wulfris back in 1665 still perpetuates her name and charitable intention in ways she could never have imagined.

A Grenadier cap of the South Hampshire Militia, 1761. Edward Gibbon provided the Latin motto, Falces conflantur in enses – 'Sickles are beaten into swords'. Gibbon was captain of the Company of Grenadiers, with J.B. Harrison as his lieutenant. This cap was presented by his grandson, Henry Austen Harrison, to the Hartley Institution and transferred in 1912 to the collection of Tudor House Museum. (Courtesy Southampton City Museums).

The Harrisons and the Ogles

The official list of Southampton thoroughfares includes three instances of "cut" designating a narrow lane or passageway and taking their names from the owners of the properties through or alongside which they ran. Other "cuts" may have names enjoying only local currency or have disappeared through redevelopment — like Aslatt's Cut, which flanked John Aslatt's coachworks at the top of Above Bar until swallowed up into Civic Centre Road half a century ago.

Of the established trio, the most recent is Western District Cut, off Shirley Road, running through the site of the schools so called when taken over in 1895 by Southampton from the Millbrook School Board which had opened them the previous year. The buildings of the former Western Schools are now used by St. Mark's Middle School and Western Adult Education Centre. By remarkable coincidence, Southampton's other two surviving 'cuts' both perpetuate the name Harrison.

In Shirley, Harrison's Cut between Winchester and Anglesea Roads keeps the memory of Jabez Harrison who established his nursery garden to the west of it in late Victorian times. The family business continued there until after World War II, when the site was sold to a garage firm.

The other Harrison's Cut lies off St. Mary Street and dates back nearly 200 years, recalling long-vanished incidents in local history and the association of successive bearers of the name John Butler Harrison with celebrities as diverse as Edward Gibbon and Jane Austen.

The beautifully detailed Ordnance Survey map of 1846 (reprinted in facsimile by the City Record Office) depicts half an acre of mature tree-girt garden, backing on to the houses of Chapel Street, with Harrison's Cut running along its northern side, linking St. Mary Street with St. Mary's Place and Hoglands — long before the advent of the A33 curtailed this walk.

With his coach house and stable at its eastern end, this land was the detached 'pleasure ground' of J.B. Harrison, who for sixty years until his death in 1850 lived in a house fronting St. Mary Street, immediately north of the cut.

The Harrison story must, however, begin with his father of the same name, who is remembered through references in the journals which the future historian Edward Gibbon (1737-94) kept for the period 1760-62 when they were fellow officers in the South Battalion of the Hampshire Militia.

(Gibbon's experiences during these years were described in an article by R. G. Whitfield, published in *Hampshire* for October 1971.)

Edward Gibbon, senior, had been M.P. for Petersfield in 1734 and for Southampton from 1741 to 1747, afterwards establishing himself as a country gentleman at Buriton, where the manor house is still to be seen as he extended it. Father and son took militia commissions, as major and captain respectively, on June 12, 1759, the same day that J. B. Harrison became a lieutenant. His family home was at Amery House, Alton.

Militia officers were usually landed gentry or men of property who volunteered as a matter of status but when other ranks were required they were conscripted through parish quotas, drawn by lot.

Although threats of French invasion virtually disappeared by the end of 1759, three dozen battalions of county militia, including the two for Hampshire, were called up for service the following May and kept 'embodied' until December 1762.

For two and a half years Gibbon and his colleagues led what he called "a wandering life of military servitude". Their "bloodless and inglorious campaigns" involved drills, exercises and ceremonial parades; marching from one set of quarters to another through the Southern counties; guarding French prisoners of war (an unpopular duty) at Portchester, Forton and elsewhere; four months in camp on the downs outside Winchester from June 1761; and the latter part of 1762 spent "at the fashionable resort of Southampton".

The officers lived well enough, devoting much of their time to eating, drinking and exchanging hospitality with local notables, mayors and corporations. Gibbon was able to pursue his studies during his frequent periods back at Buriton or when he could take private lodgings — he got very good ones in the High Street, Southampton, at a guinea a week in August, 1762.

He nevertheless took his soldiering seriously. In June, 1761 a Company of Grenadiers was formed, with Gibbon as its captain and Harrison as his lieutenant. They seem to have made it an efficient firing force.

Gibbon found the company of his fellow officers generally uncongenial — "my temper was insensibly soured by the society of rustic officers" having "no manners, no conversation" — but he made an exception of Jack Harrison, with whom he formed his one real friendship at this time. He confided to his journal "Harrison is a young man of honor, spirit and good nature. The virtues of his heart make amends for his not having those of the head."

Gibbon several times invited him to Buriton. They went to church together and dined on venison, sent from his Sussex estate at Up Park by Sir Matthew Featherstonhaugh, M.P. for Portsmouth. Harrison stayed three or four days with Gibbon in July, 1762 but Gibbon privately regretted not being able to get back to his books. "Civility (tho' we were intimate) would not let me leave Harrison, so that I was forced to lounge about with him all day; . . . when our common topicks about the Battalion were exhausted, he has not sufficient acquaintance with books or with the world to find any other." The next "was an exact copy of the preceding day" but on the third "Harrison rode out with my father so that I had some moments to myself" (for studying a French bibliography).

In August the battalion settled itself in Southampton. Lieut. Harrison marched there with 40 recruits from Petersfield whereas Major and Captain Gibbon travelled by coach.

"Bumperising till after roll call" and similar entries are frequent in Gibbon's journal over the following weeks. On September 29 he had to record "We drank a vast deal too much wine today and had a most disagreeable proof of the pernicious consequences of it; I quarrelled when I was drunk with my good friend Harrison (the Lord knows for what) and had not some of the Company been sober, it might have been a very serious affair." Next day he was happy to add "As soon as I had slept off the fumes of the wine I settled everything in an amicable way with Harrison."

The long awaited disbanding of the militia came just before Christmas. At Alton on December 18 Captain Gibbon "gave the men some beer at roll calling, which they received with great cheerfullness and decency. I dined and lay at Harrison's, where I was received with that old-fashioned breeding, which is at once so honorable and so troublesome."

On December 30, 1762, Gibbon had a sad event to note: "We received the news of poor Tom Harrison's death which sincerely affected us. About ten days before I had left him at Alton perfectly well. He was taken a very bad smallpox which carried him off in a few days. He was a worthy brother of Jack Harrison. With a temper somewhat rougher, he possessed an equal fund of honor and probity."

Thomas Harrison had joined the Hampshire militia as an ensign only twelve months before his untimely death.

Edward Gibbon had connections with Southampton through his father having been its M.P. in the 1740's. Like the latter in 1734, he himself was elected an honorary burgess of the town in October, 1762. Following his militia service, Gibbon spent two years on the continent but kept in touch with Harrison, although his letters led the scholar to "ponder regretfully on the illiteracy of this good fellow". Gibbon retained his militia commission until 1770, attending from 1765 the month-long exercises held at Southampton each Spring, until he became disenchanted with their "tiresome repetition" and the boorish officers, who no longer included J.B. Harrison.

Harrison may have settled in Southampton around 1765, for the Corporation Journal records his election as a burgess in September, 1766 (during the mayoralty of Henry Hartley, the wine merchant whose eccentric son later left the family fortune to establish the Institution that afterwards became the University of Southampton).

John Butler Harrison was descended from Thomas Harrison who in 1670 had married Elizabeth, daughter of Daniel Butler, of Amery House, Alton, which his father had bought in 1635. The parish registers of Holy Rood contain a sequence of poignant entries involving J.B. Harrison, beginning with his marriage on July 2, 1764 to Elizabeth Ballard, daughter of Rev. Dr. J. Ballard, who then held a living in Wiltshire but came of an old Southampton family. She died the following May, still only 18, three days after the birth of a daughter (christened Elizabeth Goring Harrison on June 14) and was buried "in Mr. Ballard's vault near the north-east pillar of the tower of Holy Rood church".

The bereaved Harrison later took a second wife. The marriage was doubly ill-fated. His wedding to Frances, eldest daughter of Alderman Robert Ballard, of Southampton, took place at Chawton on August 12, 1766; within a year both were to be interred at Holy Rood.

The *Salisbury Journal* of April 20, 1767 reported the death: "On Sunday morning last at Southampton of John Butler Harrison, a gentleman of handsome fortune and captain of the Hampshire Militia; being of a very amiable disposition and a person of much worth, his death is universally lamented."

Edward Gibbon was keenly affected by Harrison's passing at the early age of 28 — like his younger brother, a victim of smallpox. On April 29, Gibbon wrote to his close friend John Holroyd (later first Earl of Sheffield): "I have been assailed by a severe shock — the loss of a friend. His feelings were tender and noble . . . his principles just and generous . . . You will excuse my having said so much of a man you had not the least knowledge of but my mind is just now so full of him that I cannot easily talk of anything else."

J.B Harrison did not live to see the birth of the son who continued his name. He was born on May 6 and only 24 days after her confinement his mother was dead — seven weeks after the death of her husband. A monument to him and "his two beloved wives" was placed in Alton church — "their great many virtues truth must acknowledge".

In 1767, Harrison was still described in the Holy Rood parish register as "of Amery in Alton" but that estate was sold while the orphaned John Butler Harrison II and his half-sister Elizabeth were being brought up by their Ballard family guardians in Southampton. Both proved sturdy enough; she lived to 84, he to 83 years.

His youth remains shadowy but presumably he received an inheritance of some substance on coming of age in 1788, when he entered the Southampton civic scene. That September he was elected a burgess and "Common Council Man", sworn in as Junior Bailiff for the ensuing year. A year later he advanced to Senior Bailiff and in October, 1790 his annual progress through the Corporation hierarchy continued with him being made Sheriff.

Harrison had only to wait until September 29, 1794 to be be elected mayor. If 27 seems young for that office, it must be remembered that the "closed" (self-perpetuating) Corporation of those days had few members — most of them already former mayors — and that the office involved considerable financial obligations in dispensing hospitality, so a new recruit willing to accept them was understandably welcome.

Harrison quickly became a man of standing in Southampton, rating an "esquire" after his name and being listed in 1793 as one of the Royal Southampton Archers, whose 120 members embraced the social elite of town and county (including Samuel Harrison the banker, who may have been a relative: see article in *Hampshire,* November 1979).

In 1789, John Butler Harrison bought his "town house" and detached garden in St. Mary Street (then known as Love Lane or Bag Row) and early the following year acquired two acres in the Hoglands, which he leased out for cultivation. His property was substantial but not particularly large; the Poor Law rateable value of his house and land was £30, plus £8 for coach house and stable, etc — half that of Samuel Harrison's "country house" at Archers Lodge.

The area around St. Mary's church was then still semi-rural and J.B. Harrison probably preferred to live in the town rather than outside it. He held the post of Comptroller/Collector of Customs for over forty years from 1803 — and probably earlier. The 1803 directory, the earliest available, also listed him as one of His Majesty's Deputy Lieutenants of the Militia, a Commissioner of the Land Tax and Receiver at the Customs House for the Merchant Seamen's Hospital. Also in 1803 Harrison was appointed one of the first Southampton Harbour Commissioners, established that year to manage and improve the port facilities.

According to the *Hampshire Advertiser* obituary of 1850, he was "most highly esteemed in the performance of his public duties".

His year as Mayor in 1794-95 must have been pleasantly uneventful. Prior to 1835, the "unreformed" Corporation undertook few of the functions of a modern municipal authority (separate boards were responsible for water supply, paving and lighting and poor relief) and its business mainly comprised the management of Corporation properties — the source of its income, since it did not levy rates.

Routine business was enlivened by numerous dinners, notably those given in acknowledgement of election as honorary burgesses. Recipients of this honour in 1794-95 included a long list of titled persons, army and navy officers and local gentry. Among them were Giles Stibbert, of Portswood House, Edward Horne, of Bevis Mount, Charles Mackett, of Clay Field, William and Valentine Fitzhugh, of Bannister's Court, David Lance (not yet of Chessel House) and Nathaniel Dance, of Cranbury, the portrait painter.

There were two Royal highlights to Harrison's mayoral year. On July 4, 1795, "The Most Illustrious Prince Frederick, Duke of York" (second son of George III) "honoured the Corporation with his presence and was elected a burgess". On September 22 a similar occasion was graced by his elder brother, the Prince of Wales — "The Most High, puissant and most Illustrious Prince George Augustus Frederick".

In September, 1811, he became Mayor for a second time. He presided over the usual run of Corporation business, dealing with rents and dues, licences and leases, bills and accounts, apprenticeships, appointment of town porters and disbursement of charity funds.

On November 23, the Mayor was "desired to provide 40 or 50 tons of potatoes to be sold to the poor at a reduced price".

The Corporation also showed its social conscience by agreeing to spend the then substantial sum of £225 on coal to be sold cheaply to the poor during the winter: it then went on to elect as burgess Prince William Henry, Duke of Clarence, (third son of George III). He duly attended on the last day of the year to receive their loyal address, "humble respects and thanks for allowing them to enrol his Royal Name".

In 1812, the Corporation was involved in a complicated case arising out of the termination of John Burridge's lease of wharf and mudlands between Chapel and Northam. He sued for breach of covenant. Mayor Harrison was requested to seek a settlement but his discussions failed to prevent Burridge pursuing his suit. The Corporation defence was to no avail for in July at Winchester Assizes Burridge was awarded £1,800 damages — to meet which the Corporation was obliged to realise funds and raise money on bonds.

August, 1812, found Harrison engaged in examining encroachments made on the approaches to the "Spaw" (Spa) by Corporation tenants, with J.D. Doswell in attendance to measure up for making out new leases.

The same month, the Marquis of Wellington was elected an honorary burgess, as were the Mayor's own two eldest sons — John Butler Harrison the younger, then of Magdalen College, Oxford and Henry Austen Harrison, of the Royal Navy Pay Office, Somerset House. No doubt their father appreciated this compliment, rounding off his second period as Mayor.

Born in 1790 and 1791 respectively, they were the first two of the ten children of his marriage in 1789 (at Chawton) with Elizabeth Matilda Austen. She was a daughter of Rev. Henry Austen, of Tonbridge, first cousin of Rev. George Austen, the father of Jane Austen. The christenings of the Harrison children between 1790 and 1809 are recorded in the parish register of St. Mary's, including Elizabeth Matilda, named after her mother in 1794. The Austen connection was extended on December 15, 1814, again at St. Mary's church, when this eldest daughter married Rev. William Austen, a clergyman in Sussex.

When Jane Austen and her family spent the years 1806-09 in Southampton, they must often have visited their cousins the Harrisons, who then had another Austen in the household, Mrs. Harrison's sister, Harriet, staying with her. The novelist's surviving letters provide only a fragmentary account of her life in Southampton but include several references to the Harrisons, of St. Mary Street.

Mrs. Harrison and two of her daughters attended a party Jane Austen gave at her house in Castle Square on a cold rainy evening in October, 1808. She thought it worth recording that "Mr. Harrison came in later and sat by the fire". At the Assembly Ball on January 24, 1809 (held at the Long Room or the Dolphin?) Jane noted that "Mr. John Harrison asked me to dance" — although not indicating whether he was the middle-aged gentleman or his son, then 18, nor whether she accepted the invitation.

John Butler Harrison the younger had been a pupil of Rev. George Whittaker, the able headmaster of the local Grammar School, whence he gained a scholarship to Winchester College in 1804. Proceeding to Magdalen College, Oxford, in 1807, he took his M.A. and B.D. degrees and continued there as a Fellow till 1833, holding various posts, including Dean of Divinity. His college then presented him to the living of Evenley in Northamptonshire, where he served until his death in 1871.

Meanwhile, his father, appointed a Justice of the Peace in 1815, was very active in charitable works associated with St. Mary's church. Following its report of the crowded services for his funeral in 1850, the *Hampshire Advertiser* wrote: "His private life was one continued effort to do good — his charity was scarcely limited by his means; his services to the parish in which he had so long lived were immense. When the change of business and other circumstances had taken from the parish those who had been accustomed to aid the curates in their assistance to the sick and needy, he remained and cheerfully met the additional demands on his charity."

The reference to "curates" was pointed, since the Rector of St. Mary's for 53 years from 1787 (when the living was given him by his father, the Bishop of Winchester) was the notorious absentee pluralist Francis North, Earl of Guilford.

In the second quarter of the 19th century the St. Mary's area was rapidly built up with congested streets of generally low quality houses for the poorer sections of the town's fast expanding population. "Gentlefolk" moved away to suburban villas, leaving the Harrisons as the last of their kind in St. Mary's.

The 1841 census recorded the septuagenarian John Butler Harrison still occupying the house he had bought in 1789, his household then including three middle-aged spinster daughters and three resident servants. Mrs. Elizabeth Harrison's absence from home on census night may have been for reasons of health; she died in 1843, aged 77. Her husband survived her by seven years. Both were buried at Jesus Chapel, Pear Tree Green; their memorial was placed in St. Mary's church.

Nine of their ten children survived them; the exception was their youngest son George who joined the Indian Army and died in 1840 on a voyage home. Charles (1797-1878) and Edward (1799-1881) remained life-long residents of Southampton, well-known figures of their time, with homes in Carlton Crescent and The Polygon. The latter was a solicitor, partner in the firm of Sharp, Harrison and Turner. The longest-lived of the family was their sister, Frances, widow of Rev. James Cary, curate of St. Mary's under the Earl of Guilford and later vicar of St. Paul's church in London Road. She died in 1892, aged 86, at Gloucester House, Brunswick Place, the home she shared with several other unmarried or widowed ladies of the Harrison family. The last of them was Mary Harrison, who came to live with her aunt after the death of her father, Rev. J.B. Harrison III, whose son, the fourth generation to bear the name, followed him in the ministry. Miss Harrison afterwards bought a house at The Polygon (which she named Evenley) and lived there until her death in 1919 at 85 ended the Harrison connections with Southampton dating back over 150 years.

John Butler Harrison II bequeathed his property (including the house adjoining his own which he had purchased in 1847) to his two eldest sons "to sell for the most moneys that could reasonably be gotten". Significantly — highlighting the changes in the St. Mary's area that had gathered pace during the preceding decades — they had to sell it all to the Guardians of the Poor, for £3,000; the conveyance dated September 19, 1850 is preserved in the Southampton Record Office.

To supplement their overcrowded old workhouse across the street (rebuilt in 1866-68 and in the 1950s enlarged and adapted to accommodate Southampton Technical College), the Guardians lost little time in using the site for the erection of Workhouse Schools, Union Dispensary and Relieving Office, with part of J.B. Harrison's former "pleasure ground" serving as playspace for the unfortunate pauper children.

In November, 1851 the Guardians tried to get a vestry meeting of St. Mary's parishioners to agree to their request for "the early stopping up of the passage

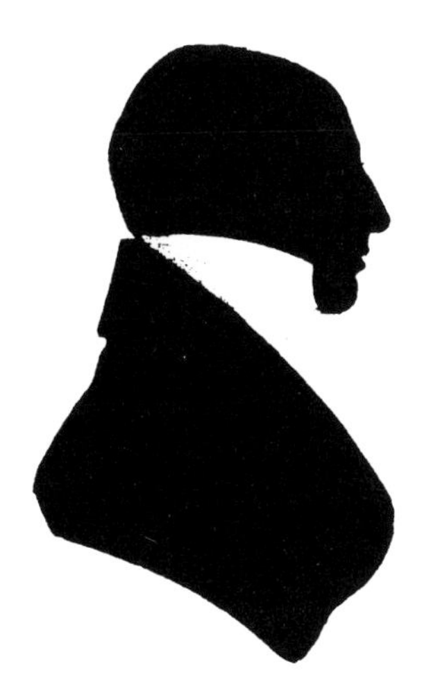

J.B Harrison
1767 – 1850

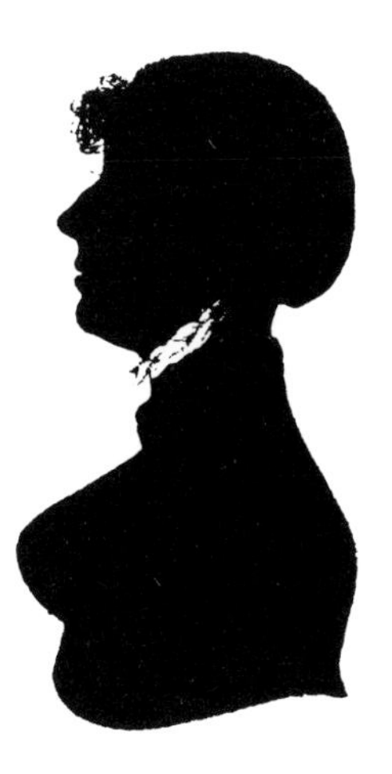

Elizabeth Harrison (nee Austen)
1766 – 1843

Elizabeth Goring Harrison
1765 – 1849

These silhouettes of John Butler Harrison II (1767-1850); his wife Elizabeth (1766-1843) and his half-sister Elizabeth Goring Harrison (1765-1849) are taken from a family album compiled by his grandson Francis Slade Harrison (1850-1926), son of Rev. William Harrison, the fifth son of J.B. Harrison II, and bequeathed to Southampton Record Office in 1986 by his daughter Helena Austen Harrison. (Courtesy Record Office.)

bisecting the schoolhouse property" and the diversion of this public way to Chapel Street, to allow them to make more intensive use of the whole site. The attempt failed because the passage between J.B. Harrison's former house and garden was already an established and convenient footpath, evidently valued by local residents.

Efforts to close it were not pursued and although the surrounding area has since seen many changes, Harrison's Cut remains firmly on the town map — 200 years after the man whose name it perpetuates first bought the house and land flanking it.

Ogle Road

Ogle Road is another Southampton thoroughfare perpetuating a distinctive personal name. Although largely unrecognised today, it was familiar enough to townspeople a century ago, when the road was built up across the site and grounds of the old 8-bedroom "town house" listed in directories as 63 Above Bar but generally known as Ogle House, after the family who lived there from 1792 to 1869.

Sold for demolition and redevelopment in 1875, it had by then become a prime central site, occupying an acre and a half to the north of Regent Street (anciently Canshut or Caneshote Lane, also Windmill Lane, the old road out of the town along the shore to the west), extending to the backs of properties in Manchester Street and from Above Bar through to Portland Terrace — where land had been kept free of buildings to preserve the fine views from the house across Southampton Water to the New Forest. As a family mansion, it had a much longer history than its tenure by the Ogles, being an early Georgian conversion of what had previously been a brewhouse and originally a farmstead dating back to Tudor times.

The forerunner of Ogle House can be identified with the "Mawdlin House and orchards" held in 1602 by George Watson, a "husbandman" or farmer who that year was among those fined ten shillings at Court Leet for "keeping Common Bowlinge allyes within there orchards contrarie to statute". Also in 1602, the town's "Book of Remembrance" recorded evidence given by Watson's wife and his two female tenants against "one Gubbin of Leeth and the wife of one Webb of Elinge" who had spent three weeks at Mawdlin House. They pretended to be cousins or brother and sister but the women deposed that, besides playing bowls in the orchard, the couple "were many times fast locked up together . . . and lived verie badly and incontinentlie". Mrs. Watson became "suspicious of their dishonest lives together" and told Gubbin not to come to her house again — "she verely beleiveth by the light behavour of the woman and the wanton toyes that she had seen between them that they lived dishonestlie together and verie dissolute".

Ogle House, Above Bar.

Southampton.—Sale of a Valuable Freehold House and Land, containing about 1¼ acres, situate in the High-street, Above Bar, and known as Miss Ogle's, in the parish of All Saints, in the centre of the flourishing town of Southampton.—To be Sold by Auction, by

MR. W. FURBER (by order of the Executors of the late Miss Ogle), at the Royal Hotel, Above Bar, Southampton, on WEDNESDAY, the 23rd of June, 1875, at 3 for 4 o'clock precisely.

To be sold with possession.

PARTICULARS.

The property consists of a DETACHED FAMILY MANSION, conveniently situated on the west side of Above Bar, in the High-street, Southampton, with stabling and extensive garden.

The residence is brick-built, with a lawn in front.

The house is approached from the High-street (from which it is screened by a fine row of lime trees) by a good carriage sweep, with two pair of folding entrance gates and iron railings, and contains the following accommodation:—Large entrance hall, drawing room, breakfast room, dining room, library, eight bedrooms, two dressing rooms, china closet, two kitchens, larder, scullery, butler's pantry, morning or smoking room, store room, w.c.; a very handsome staircase, 4ft. wide, with massive oak balustrades.

The rooms are well fitted with cupboards, shelves, &c.

The cellarage is very superior, extending under the whole house, and comprise coal cellar, wine cellars fitted with bins, &c.

The stabling consists of a yard with separate entrance from the street, five-stall stable, double coachhouse, water closet, and loft over.

The pleasure grounds, in which there is a greenhouse, are extensive, and contain about 1¼ acres of land, extending from the High-street to Upper Portland-terrace, and there is a right of way over the roads shown on the plan which precludes the erection of buildings on the piece of land coloured green on the plan, and thereby affords a view from the mansion of the Southampton Water and the New Forest.

The property is well worth the attention of speculators, and is capable of being developed to great advantage as building land.

It contains above 1¼ acres, and has a frontage to the High-street of 164ft. or thereabouts, and a depth of 406ft., and from its situation in the principal thoroughfare of a large and important town, would afford an excellent site for a Townhall, Bank, or other Public Institution, or for the erection of a Theatre, Lecture Hall, or Aquarium, or of Assembly or Club Rooms, either in combination with shops or otherwise; or the land is capable of being sub-divided and laid out for building purposes, and is of sufficient width to give double frontages of upwards of 400ft., with a uniform depth of 66ft., on a new street of the width of 32ft., extending from the High-street to Upper Portland-terrace, thus affording excellent sites for the erection of shops, or of houses for occupation as private residences or professional offices.

The house contains a large quantity of most excellent building materials.

All fixtures on the premises are included in the sale.

May be viewed on application at the house, and particulars had of Messrs. E. and H. Tylee, Wickham and Moberly, solicitors, 14, Essex-street, Strand, London, W.C.; Messrs. Westbury and Sons, land agents and surveyors, Andover; or at the office of Mr. Wm. Furber, the auctioneer, 22, Above Bar, Southampton.

Apart from this amorous episode, the earliest surviving documentation is a conveyance of 1670 in the City Record Office relating to the sale for £400 by a London grocer, Thomas Randall, to the Southampton merchant William Stanley of several properties, the chief of which were "the capital messuage and brewhouse commonly called The Old Brewhouse", with yards, gardens, orchards, stables and other outbuildings, along with a barn and five acres of meadow lying behind them.

The brewer tenant then and earlier was George Embree, who remained until his death in 1678. He was afterwards followed by John Normanton, who married the widow Cordelia Embree in 1683. They were prominent members of the Society of Friends, whose meetings were held at the house — in secret. Until granted toleration in 1687-89, Quakers (originally a jeering misnomer) faced prosecution for not attending Anglican services at their parish church and were liable to fines and imprisonment for gathering privately in illegal "conventicles" for their own form of worship.

"Captain Embree's conventicle" was often raided and he, Normanton and others attending, were several times sentenced to pay substantial fines, exacted by distraint on their property, or sent to prison for their persistence, compounded by refusal to doff their hats in front of the magistrates. George Embree was also prosecuted for unlawful preaching: Quaker marriages took place at his house. Styled "Captain" from his service in Cromwell's army, he was evidently a man of resolution and some substance, a carrier and soap maker as well as a brewer. On behalf of the Friends, he bought in 1662 (paying £10 for a 1,000 year title) a "cabbidge plot" of 68 by 62 ft. "on the west side of the road from Southton to Winton and to the north of the Common gate", to serve as a burial ground. He was one of the first to be laid to rest there, 16 years later. Enlarged in 1841, this little tree-lined cemetery with its uniformly simple memorials is still a feature of The Avenue, behind a red brick wall and gate pillars unobtrusively inscribed "Society of Friends Burial Ground A.D. 1662" (between today's Archers Road and Brighton Road).

George Embree was the victim of a disastrous fire in 1672, and the Friends throughout the Southern area raised generous subscriptions for him, as also for fellow members suffering fines and distraints. Land tax lists for house and brewery (then valued at £15) show John Normanton in occupation at least until 1718. In 1722 William Stanley's heirs sold to Thomas Dummer "all that brewhouse lately converted into a dwelling house" and its various "appurtenances", together with four acres of arable land.

Conversion — doubtless followed by further alterations and enlargements — evidently produced a substantial Georgian residence suitable for "persons of quality", a succession of whom owned or leased it over the ensuing decades. Their names are recorded in contemporary tax lists and the Poor Law rate books of All Saints parish, which show it to have been one of the highest valued in Southampton. The town developed its attractions as a residential resort before it entered its "Spa period" which further enhanced them. It was particularly favoured by retired Navy and Army officers.

At the house in Above Bar, "Widow Ramonden" of the 1720s was followed by Captain Lawrence a decade later, then Captain John Towry from 1743. Member of a family pursuing naval careers through several generations, he was advanced to Admiral by mid-century but died in 1757 and his widow did not long remain at the house, for in 1759 her name was replaced by the quaint entry "Esq. Gore" — later expanded to "Charles Gore Esq." He left Southampton in 1773 and the next year the house was taken by General Lawrence, one of a long-serving Army family and perhaps the same who had lived there thirty years previously.

Lady Copley added titled lustre to the place in 1780-82, after which the house stood empty for two years before its occupation in 1784-89 by Captain Caldwell. He may be identified with Sir Benjamin Caldwell (1739-1820), who began his naval career at Portsmouth in 1754, was paid off in 1783 but later returned to active service and reached the rank of Rear Admiral in 1793. He died at his son's home in Basingstoke.

Perhaps the most interesting of these 18th century residents was Charles Gore. Born in 1729, he was the only son of a prosperous Lincolnshire merchant. In 1751, he married the daughter of a wealthy Scarborough rope-maker and her marriage portion of £40,000 enabled him to give up working in his uncle's London counting house. His father's death in 1754 brought him most of the family estate and thereafter Gore was free to indulge his mechanical and artistic talents, studying navigation and making ship models.

For these interests, as well as for the sake of his wife's health, he moved to Southampton in 1759, taking a lease of the Above Bar house which afforded views of Southampton Water. His daughter Emilie later recalled:

"Southampton from its vicinity to Portsmouth and to Spithead afforded him all he could wish for the study of his favourite object which he indefatigably pursued for ten or twelve years, amusing himself with the construction of different vessels after his own models, one of which (the *Snail* cutter), remarkable for her elegance of form and swiftness of sailing, was well known and admired by the Navy. Mr. Gore had many times the honour to carry His Majesty's brothers the Dukes of York, Gloucester and Cumberland in his cutter from Southampton to Spithead, Portsmouth, the Isle of Wight etc. He generally passed his summers and indeed most of the year in different excursions with the Fleet around the coasts of England, France, the Channel Islands etc."

From 1773 Gore undertook extensive travels through western Europe with his wife and daughters, spending much time sketching and painting. His wife died in 1785 and after six more years of nomadic life Gore finally settled in Germany.

He became a friend of Goethe (the model for the much-travelled and cultivated Englishman in his novel "The Elective Affinities") and of Duke Karl August of Saxe-Weimar. Gore and his daughters came to occupy a central position at the Ducal court in Weimar, then a centre of artistic and intellectual activities which Gore enhanced after having a house built there in 1793. His extensive library and art collection were happily spared when French troops ransacked it in 1806 but the looting of his home hastened Gore's death the following January.

Some 1,500 of his paintings and drawings are preserved in the Goethe National Museum at Weimar, where the Library displays the bust of their friend which the Duke and Goethe commissioned C.G. Weisser to make.

Gore was surprisingly omitted from the Dictionary of National Biography but has been the subject of an essay by R.C.B. Oliver (Radnorshire Society Transactions, 1977).

Rating a two-page entry in the D.N.B. is a man of lesser talent who lived in the same Southampton house for about three years from 1789. William Sotheby (1757-1833) was the eldest son of a Guards officer who had married a daughter of William Sloane, of South Stoneham. He began an army career but in 1780 he "increased his resources" by marrying a Northamptonshire heiress. "Thereupon he retired from the army and purchasing the residence of Bevis Mount, near Southampton, settled down with every material advantage to a literary life."

He devoted himself to the classics but his first publication in 1790 was a volume of poems, mostly narrating a walking tour of Wales made with his brother in 1788. On his return, he seems to have quitted Bevis Mount for the more modest mansion in Above Bar, from which he removed to London. There he quickly became prominent in literary circles, friendly with most of the celebrated authors of his day and helpful to aspiring young writers. He gained a literary reputation through his translations from German and classic literature but was less esteemed for his own prolific output of poems and five-act historical tragedies in blank verse. His close friendships included Sir Walter Scott and Lord Byron who once said that Sotheby "has imitated everybody and occasionally surpassed his models".

In 1822, he delivered an eloquent address to the Dilettante Society, of which he had been a leading member since 1792, on the death of his friend, the antiquarian Sir Henry Englefield — best remembered as author of "A Walk Through Southampton". A road at Bitterne Manor was named after him in 1902 (see *Streets*, page 89).

Throughout the 18th century the Above Bar mansion seems to have lacked a distinctive name. Only later did it become known as Ogle House. The Ogle connection began in 1792 when it was leased by Captain Chaloner Ogle, R.N.

In 1805 he paid £4,500 to buy the property from the heirs of Col. William Baynard, its previous owner, and continued living there until his death in 1814. Little is known of him but he bore the name of an extensive family, with numerous members prominent in navy and church, which originated in Northumberland but was also established in Hampshire.

Sir William Ogle had held Winchester castle for the King in 1643-45, until forced to yield it to Parliament's forces, and in the early 19th century there were several Ogles living around Southampton. Little Testwood House was "the seat of H. Ogle Esq.": Nathaniel Ogle of Millbrook is remembered as the partner of W.A. Summers, pioneering steam-driven road carriages at Foundry Lane. Captain Ogle may have been related to them and his two more celebrated namesakes, both admirals. The first, Sir Chaloner Ogle (1681-1750), was knighted for his part in capturing pirate ships off Africa in 1722, when the notorious buccaneer Bartholomew Roberts was killed. His widow, Lady Isabella Ogle, married the fourth Lord Kingston, who settled at Worthy House (north of Winchester) in 1752. On their deaths in 1761, this property passed to another Chaloner Ogle (1727-1816) who extended the estate by purchasing the manors of Martyr Worthy and Kings Worthy in 1773.

His naval services eventually brought the reward of a baronetcy, beginning the peerage which became extinct in 1940. He married Hesther, daughter of Rev. Dr. John Thomas, Bishop of Winchester in 1761-81. His brother, Dr. Newton Ogle (1726-1804), married another daughter of the same bishop — his eldest, Susannah — and received several ecclesiastical preferments. He was Dean of Winchester from 1769 until his death and Rector of St. Mary's, Southampton from 1776 until 1797, when he resigned in favour of the pluralist Francis North, later Earl of Guilford. Dr. Ogle being already Dean of Winchester when appointed Rector of St. Mary's explains why its rectory came to be known as "The Deanery". He had a family of nine children, the youngest of whom, Esther Jane, was married at St. Mary's in 1795 to R.B. Sheridan, the famous dramatist and statesman.

After the death of Captain Chaloner Ogle, the estate in Above Bar passed to his widow, Catherine, and on her death in 1820 to her two daughters, Charlotte and Catherine. They remained unmarried and spent their long lives at Ogle House. These must have been quietly uneventful. The only documentation surviving relates to their purchase of plots of land in 1835 and 1842 to enlarge their garden and prevent building in Portland Terrace spoiling their water and forest views. The 1851 census recorded them at home, respectively aged 70 and 69, both born at Winchester and described on the schedule as "gentlewomen" and "fund-holders" i.e. living on dividends from investments. They were served by four resident servants — cook, ladies' maid, housemaid and butler. All four were still at Ogle House in 1861 with Miss Charlotte but her younger sister had died about 1853. The elder Miss Ogle died in 1869.

Having presumably outlived any likely relatives, she bequeathed all her property to two clergymen, Rev. Charles Randolph of Kimpton (who died in 1871) and Rev. Christopher Fawcett of Somerford Keynes, on trust to sell at their discretion. Rather surprisingly, it remained in the market for several years, until eventually "the valuable freehold house with stabling and extensive pleasure grounds containing above one and a half acres, situated in the centre of the flourishing town of Southampton" was put up for auction by William Furber at the Royal Hotel in Above Bar on June 23, 1875.

The sales particulars described the "detached family mansion" in some detail — "screened from the road by a fine row of lime trees and approached by a good carriage sweep, with two pairs of folding entrance gates and iron railings", it contained "large entrance hall, drawing room, breakfast room, dining room, library, eight bedrooms, two dressing rooms, china closet, two kitchens, larder, scullery, butler's pantry, morning or smoking room, store room, w.c.; a very handsome staircase, 4 ft. wide, with massive oak balustrades"; there was "very superior cellarage, extending under the whole house" and in a yard with separate entrance from the street were a five-stall stable and a double coach-house, with loft over it. More pointedly, since no-one was expected to want to open up the old house again as a private residence, the auctioneer underlined that "the house contains a large quantity of most excellent building materials" and "the property is well worth the attention of speculators and is capable of being developed to great advantage as building land".

As local papers reported, "it was knocked down for £4,550 to Mr. Harry Coles of Bridge Street after a sharp competition between a number of well-known capitalists". Coles made a quick profit of £700 by selling it the following January to Charles A. Day of Terrace House, Polygon and the firm of Day, Summers and Co. He had the estate divided up into building plots flanking a new road cut through the estate — for which Ogle Road was the obvious choice of name.

The sales particulars had not failed to mention that the property "would afford an excellent site for a Town Hall, Bank or other Public Institution". Southampton certainly needed a new centre of municipal administration to replace the old Audit House in the High Street, which was widely condemned as inadequate and inconvenient, "a disgrace to the town". The Corporation missed the chance of buying it before or at auction and in 1877 twice rejected the opportunity to acquire all or part of the Ogle House site — much to the disgust of its forward-looking surveyor, James Lemon, who later wrote in his Reminiscences "I cannot help thinking this is one of the greatest blunders the Corporation ever made". The vexed "Town Hall question" was to remain the subject of much indecisive discussion in both town and borough council over the next fifty years, until eventually agreement was reached, largely through the initiative and persistence of Sir Sidney Kimber, to use the Marlands site for the erection of a modern Civic Centre, built in stages over the years 1929-39.

Another Ogle House – a surviving example of late 19th century architecture in Ogle Road – the Sunday School hall erected in 1897 as an addition to the Church of Christ, later Above Bar Church. (Photograph: Ivan Champion).

The first building erected on the Ogle House site was a skating rink and circus, followed within a few years by more permanent buildings along Ogle Road. In 1878 a plot at the south-east corner was purchased by Timothy Coop of Wigan, who largely financed the building in 1880-81 of the Church of Christ — founded in 1876 by the Anglo-American evangelist Henry Samuel Earl, who held mission services in the adjoining Philharmonic Hall (the site of the later Odeon cinema). Church members helped to demolish Ogle House; some of its walls, nearly 3 ft. thick at the base, yielded bricks which were cleaned and re-used, while oak beams were re-worked to provide church fittings and furniture. Renamed Above Bar Church in 1954, the church itself was demolished in 1979 and rebuilt in modern style, incorporating ground floor shops, but beside it still stands the "Ogle House" of 1897, erected as a Sunday School hall.

Modern office blocks have replaced most of the original late Victorian architecture of Ogle Road, like the wholesale grocery warehouse of G.K. Page and Sons, which disappeared in 1957. Thirty years later, redevelopment brought the demolition of the building originally erected as the headquarters of the Gordon Boys' Brigade, for which the foundation stone was laid on August 10, 1889, by Princess Beatrice, accompanied by Prince Henry of Battenberg. The stone medallions adorning its frontage had included one inscribed "Gordon — Semper Fidelis". As a "parcel delivery and emigration agency" the Brigade provided a corps of uniformed messengers and helped poor boys to find new opportunities overseas. It closed down in 1939, when its Gordon mementoes were transferred to the collection of the Gordon Boys' School near Woking, established in 1885 by public subscription as a national memorial to General Gordon, directly promoted by Queen Victoria.

Portswood holds a little-known relic of the old house occupied by Captain Chaloner Ogle and his daughters. When it was demolished, the pairs of gates from its elliptical carriage drive off Above Bar were secured by Walter Perkins, who had them placed in Portswood Road, at the entrances to his own residence, Portswood House. In 1912, when that estate was being developed for housing, the gates were removed and re-positioned — one pair at the house near Lymington belonging to his son, Frank W. Perkins, the other at the entrance to the tennis courts and residents' gardens in Abbotts Way (illustrated in *Streets*, page 44). Apart from the nameplates of Ogle Road, these twice relocated gates are now the only visible reminders of the "mansion" which vanished from the Above Bar scene over a century ago.

The former headquarters of the Gordon Boys' Brigade in Ogle Road, demolished in 1987. Below: the foundation stone of the building, laid in 1889 by H.R.H. Princess Beatrice. (Photographs: Ivan Champion).

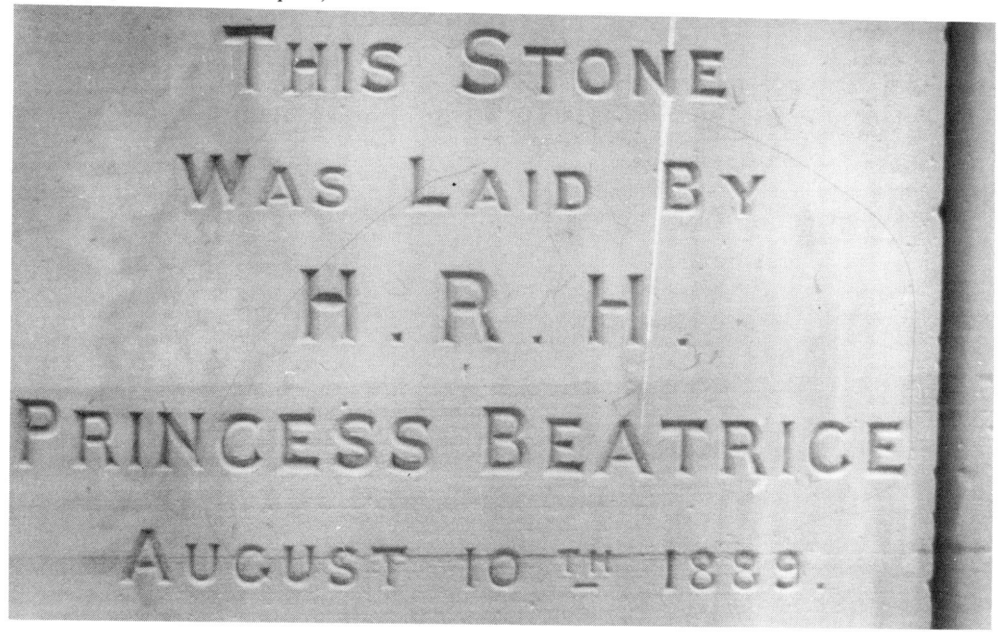

PARTICULARS

AND

CONDITIONS of SALE

OF

A Spacious Elegant New-Built Freehold HOUSE,

With DOUBLE COACH HOUSE,

STABLING for EIGHT HORSES,

Numerous Attached and Detached OFFICES

Of every Defcription,

Suited to the *VILLA* and the *ORNAMENTED FARM.*

EXCELLENT KITCHEN GARDENS

Surrounded with Lofty Walls,

DIVIDED and SUBDIVIDED, richly CLOATHED with a SELECTION of FRUIT TREES in FULL BEARING.

PLEASURE GROUND *Disposed with great Taste;*

AND

Beautiful PADDOCK of about Thirty Acres;

Together with, (at a SUITABLE DISTANCE from the Houfe,)

A SMALL FARM HOUSE, BARN, GRANERY, DOVE COTE, and RICH MEADOWS,

Making with the above, about FORTY-EIGHT *ACRES,*

Within a RING FENCE;

VALUABLE RIGHT on SHIRLEY COMMON, &c.

Called

SHIRLEY HOUSE;

Beautifully Situate *within Two Miles of* SOUTHAMPTON,

IN

The COUNTY of HANTS.

Which will be SOLD by AUCTION

BY

Mr. CHRISTIE,

At his Great Room in *Pall Mall,* on WEDNESDAY the 6th of JUNE 1792, at One o'Clock.

Shirley, Hollybrook and Millbrook

Richville Road, laid out by 1897 and built up from 1902, was named with a touch of fanciful French elegance to carry a reminder of the titled owner a century earlier of the "big house" across whose grounds it was laid out — echoed by Park Street and Shirley Park Road, which date from the first phase of "development" of the Shirley House estate in mid-Victorian times. The house itself stood in the area of present Clarendon and Henty Roads, with grounds of about 48 acres (Shirley Park) extending north of what is now Oakley Road towards Tanners Brook and Shirley High Street.

This eighteenth century country "mansion" was probably erected over the cellars of an older manor house, about 1760. Its first recorded occupier and the man for whom it was probably built was Richard Wilson (1725-78), who had been a plantation owner in the West Indies, on the island of St. Christopher (St. Kitts) and had there acquired the means to retire to England and establish an estate on the then outskirts of Southampton.

While in the West Indies, Wilson had married Mary Feuilleteau, four years his junior, born on St. Kitts, presumably of French (perhaps Huguenot) origin. She did not live long to enjoy her new home at Shirley House, for she died on June 14, 1764, in her 35th year — recalled as "a lady of exemplary piety and virtue" on a memorial tablet erected on the chancel wall of St. Nicholas, the former parish church of Millbrook. This also recorded the death of her daughter, Mary Susanna, on March 24, 1765, aged nine months, so Mrs. Wilson may have died in childbirth.

Her first child, born in the West Indies, was Lewis Feuilleteau Wilson (1752-1804), who went to America at the age of 21 to study at the college that later became Princeton University. His descendants in the United States still use Feuilleteau as a middle name. Robert Wilson took a second wife, Christian Gilbert, at Millbrook in November, 1764. Sadly, she died the following June. The register of St. Michael's records the third marriage of "Robert Wilson Esq. of Millbrook, widower" to Ann Serle of that parish, on November 21, 1765. This union was blessed with two sons — presumably twins — born in 1767 and named Renault Serle and Charles; the latter lived only three years.

Richard Wilson evidently maintained a "town house" as well as his country estate at Shirley. His will of 1777 bore a London address (Charlotte Street, in the County of Middlesex) and as his burial is not recorded in Southampton, his death in 1778 probably occurred there.

The subsequent occupation of Shirley House is unclear, although it may have been the home of a John Bradshaw for a few years before "this elegant new-built freehold house, beautifully situate within two miles of Southampton" was put up for sale by auction on June 6, 1792 at Mr. Christie's "Great Room in Pall Mall".

His particulars described in enthusiastic detail "the premises . . . distinguished in point of Beauty of Situation; the Mansion, remarkable for its simple Elegance of Architectural Elevation and internal Proportion of Apartments, correspondently finished (whatever that meant!) . . . seated on an Eminence from which the grounds are beautifully sloped and fringed with rich Plantations, looking over country replete with Objects intersecting a Mass of prolific Richness."

The ground floor, approached by a flight of steps with circular portico, contained spacious hall, morning, eating and drawing rooms, with principal and back staircases of stone — and a patent water closet, then by no means a usual feature even of country mansions. On the first floor were "four capital bed chambers and two neat dressing rooms"; the attics contained five neat bed chambers and two dressing rooms ("neat" always seems to have meant "small" in the property market). Besides the "spacious well fitted up kitchen", scullery, larder and other stores, butler's pantry and housekeeper's room, there were "most excellent cellars for every purpose."

The "detached offices" included a neat dairy, wash house, laundry, brew and bake house, with servants' bed chambers over them; stabling for eight horses and a double coach house, with lofts. Other features of the estate were the "kitchen gardens abundantly productive, surrounded with lofty walls; fruit trees in full bearing; Pleasure Ground disposed with great taste; beautiful paddock of about thirty acres and meadows in high Cultivation and remarkably Rich", together with, "at a suitable distance from the House, a neat Farm House, Farm Yard, Barn, Stable, Granery, Dove Cote etc." — in all, 48 acres, set within a ring fence. The estate was thus largely self-sufficient; as Mr. Christie put it, "The Offices are fully competent and judiciously disposed, possessing every requisite convenience suited to a large family." Finally, "its Locality to the capital Fish Market of Southampton renders the Whole a most desirable Residence."

Shirley House was taken by William Fulke Greville, of whom little beyond his aristocratic name seems to be recorded in Southampton. Nor was the house mentioned in early guides for visitors, issued from 1768 onwards. It was first noted in the 1795 edition of Baker's "Southampton Guide" — as "the first object that strikes us on the Romsey road . . . the seat of William Greville Esq., a pleasant situation not far from the road side. The gardens are neat and extensive and the house commands a variety of prospects".

In 1802 Shirley House became the home of Rev. Sir Charles Rich, who for the previous four years had leased Grove Place, Nursling. He was originally Rev. Charles Bostock, a member of an old Cheshire family who in 1783 married

Mary Frances Rich, only daughter and heir of Lieut. General Sir Robert Rich, fifth baronet in a lineage traced back to the fifteenth century. The general died in 1785 and was succeeded by his bachelor brother, George, on whose death in 1799 the baronetcy would have become extinct but for Mr. Bostock having assumed the surname Rich in 1790 and being himself created a baronet in 1791.

Sir Charles Bostock Rich lived at Shirley House until his death in 1824 and was doubtless responsible for improving and enlarging it in Regency style. The house was noteworthy among several of its kind then surrounding Southampton, being appreciatively noted by guidebook writers for the attention of visitors frequenting the town — no longer a fashionable spa but still appealing to the well-to-do as a "genteel resort" offering pleasant coach drives around it.

Baker's "Southampton Guide" of 1804 informed them that "on the Romsey Road the first conspicuous object is Shirley House, the property of Rev. Sir Charles Rich, bart. It is a substantial modern mansion and commands a variety of prospects".

To preserve his southerly "prospects" the reverend baronet leased from the lord of the manor, Sir Charles Mill, of Mottisfont, several plots of arable and meadow land, which he happily undertook to maintain "according to the most usual and best approved methods of husbandry". They covered some 34 acres, south of Oakley Road and west of Waterhouse Lane — crossed by the upper part of Regents Park Road in the 1840s.

Oakley Road was then known as Mousehole Lane, described on the plans attached to Sir Charles Rich's leases of 1802-03 as leading "from the Mill to the Common" or "from Mousehole and Waste to the Common" i.e. Shirley Common, which was not enclosed and allotted to individual owners until 1830. Mousehole Mill was then a corn mill (as shown on the first Ordnance Survey map of 1806), driven by the water power of Tanners Brook — or rather the straight mill race cut down from Old Shirley beside it, leaving the reduced stream meandering along to the east until the two joined again just below Mousehole Mill. By 1843, the mill had become a foundry, run for twenty years by Benjamin Peach Napier, "iron founder and machine manufacturer"; he was followed by other ironmasters until Mousehole Foundry ceased operations in late Victorian times.

In 1909, when "prospects" around Mousehole Lane were greatly altered from a century before, local residents petitioned the borough council to change what they evidently felt was an inappropriate name for an Edwardian residential area. They suggested "Burlington Road", a famous London name with aristocratic associations, but this had already been earmarked for one of the roads being laid out across the old Terrace House estate by the Newcombe Estates Company. When the matter was referred to a sub-committee, it was decided, on the motion of the Sheriff, seconded by the Senior Bailiff, that Mousehole Lane should be re-styled Oakley Road. On July 28 the Council confirmed the new name: chairing its meeting was the Mayor, Councillor Richard Garrett Oakley, in compliment to whom the new name was adopted.

He had represented Bevois ward for four years, re-elected unopposed in 1908 a few days before being chosen mayor. Although a comparative newcomer on the civic scene, Oakley came of a family long established in Southampton. His business as fruit merchant and shipping contractor derived from his family's earlier occupations of farmers and nurserymen. R. G. Oakley's great-grandfather had cultivated land in the Newtown area; his grandfather had a cherry orchard where the jail in Ascupart Street was built in 1855; his father bought a field in Kingsland and used its clay for brick-making. In his mayoral year Richard Oakley opened the "new" Girls' Grammar School in Argyle Road, gave trees to improve Queen's Park and visited every Council school in the borough, besides presiding at 21 council meetings and attending 104 committees. Perhaps the busy mayor merited commemoration on the street map — which fortuitously avoided the problem of duplication arising when another Mousehole Lane at Bitterne was brought within the borough by the boundary extension of 1920.

Waterhouse Lane bears a distinctive name — older than Foundry Lane and early Victorian Regents Park Road, between which it has led down to Millbrook Road for more than two centuries. Its name was evidently well established by 1817, when the parish register of St. Nicholas (the old church that stood on the south side of Millbrook Road, opposite the bottom of Regents Park Road, superseded by Holy Trinity in 1874 but not demolished until 1939) recorded the baptism of "Mary, daughter of Edward and Frances Newman, Waterhouse Lane, gardener".

It is tempting to associate the lane with the stream, now reduced to a drain, which ran from the Church Street/Salem Street area roughly parallel with it to the west, through the grounds of former "Blighmont" Farm, House and Lodge, to the pre-reclamation waterline across Millbrook Road. It is, of course, possible that there was at some time a "waterhouse" along this stream, where local folk may have drawn water or washed clothes, but, if so, it was never significant enough to be marked on any surviving map or to receive contemporary notice.

The maps identifying the land leased by Sir Charles Rich in 1802-03 indicate another, hitherto unrecognised, origin for Waterhouse Lane — as a variant or corruption of the earlier Watt House or Wathouse Lane. One of the Rich leases was for 14 years from Michaelmas 1802 for "all that messuage, tenement, barn, yard, garden and buildings known by the name of Watt House, together with seven pieces of arable and meadow land thereunto belonging". Three of the plots named on the plans accompanying this and other leases (preserved

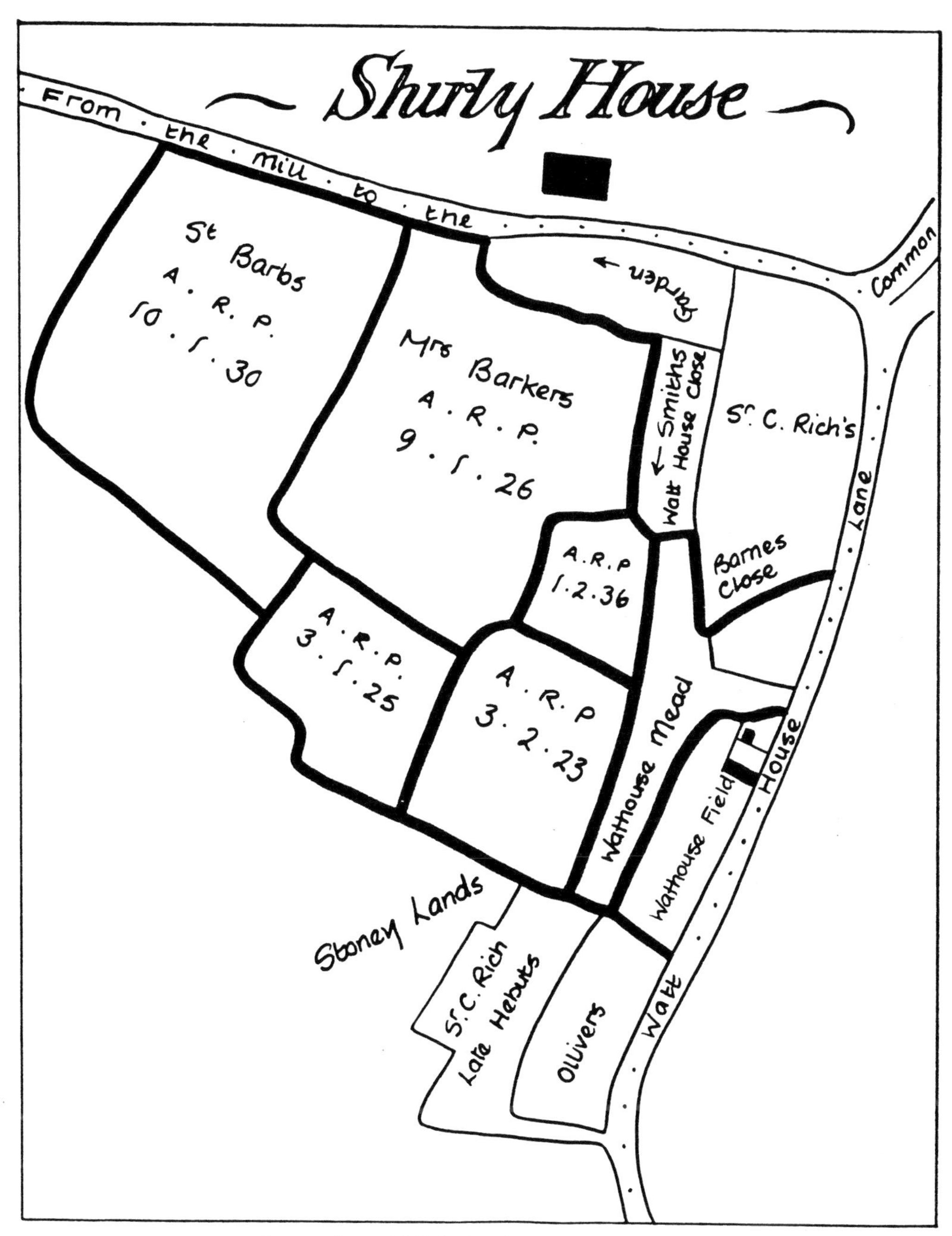

Lease plan of 1802 showing Watt House Lane.
(From the original in Southampton Record Office).

in Southampton Record Office) were Wathouse Mead, Wathouse Field and Watt House Close, all off the western side of the lane, adjoining each other around the buildings fronting the lane, also styled Wathouse or Watt House.

The lawyer preparing these agreements probably followed the terms of earlier leases, repeating the original names that may already have been superseded in popular usage. "Wathouse or Waterhouse Lane" (running south from what was then called Shirley Lane i.e. Mousehole Lane/Oakley Road) was clearly marked on an older map of "the leasehold farms in the manor of Millbrook belonging to Rev. Mr. Jones", also held in the Record Office. This is undated but was probably drawn about 1750-60. It shows plots designated Wathouse and St. Barb's, continuing to bear the names of previous holders. Since parish registers before 1812 did not usually note addresses or occupations, one can now only speculate about the identity of the Mr. Watt who may have given his name to a farm house and fields, transferred to the lane they flanked — its origin afterwards lost and forgotten under the form in which Waterhouse Lane has so long been known.

Following the death of Sir Charles Rich in 1824, his widow, Dame Mary Frances Rich, remained at Shirley House until shortly before her death in 1833. In 1835 her son and heir, Sir Charles Henry Rich (1784-1857) sold the estate for £11,850 to a local syndicate including William Henry Roe, who in 1853 became its sole owner. He was a builder and surveyor, with a house in Portland Terrace, who prospered in extending the business started by his father, Henry Roe. The Southampton directory of 1811 listed him as a carpenter in East Street; by 1834 the entry was "Roe and Son, 182 High Street", epitomising the successful careers of several builders who contributed to the expansion of Southampton.

Shirley House was leased by Major General Sleigh through the 1840s but became empty about 1852, when W. H. Roe advertised "this beautiful residence to be let or sold". He "most respectfully submitted it to the attention of Ladies and Gentlemen as a commodious, healthy and economical abode." Roe's notice and accompanying engraving indicated that the house had been enlarged since 1792, for it was now described as having two spacious drawing rooms instead of one, with a boudoir and "seven handsome bedrooms" on the floor above and "eight spacious and airy bedrooms" on the top floor.

Roe offered the house with 3, 5 or any other number of acres up to 45 (part being the dairy farm) but he eventually let it with about 12 acres to Rev. H. N. Burrows, who conducted a private school there until 1859. Sampson Payne was among those to whom, from 1852 onwards, Roe sold building plots along Shirley Park Road, laid out across the eastern part of the former Shirley House grounds.

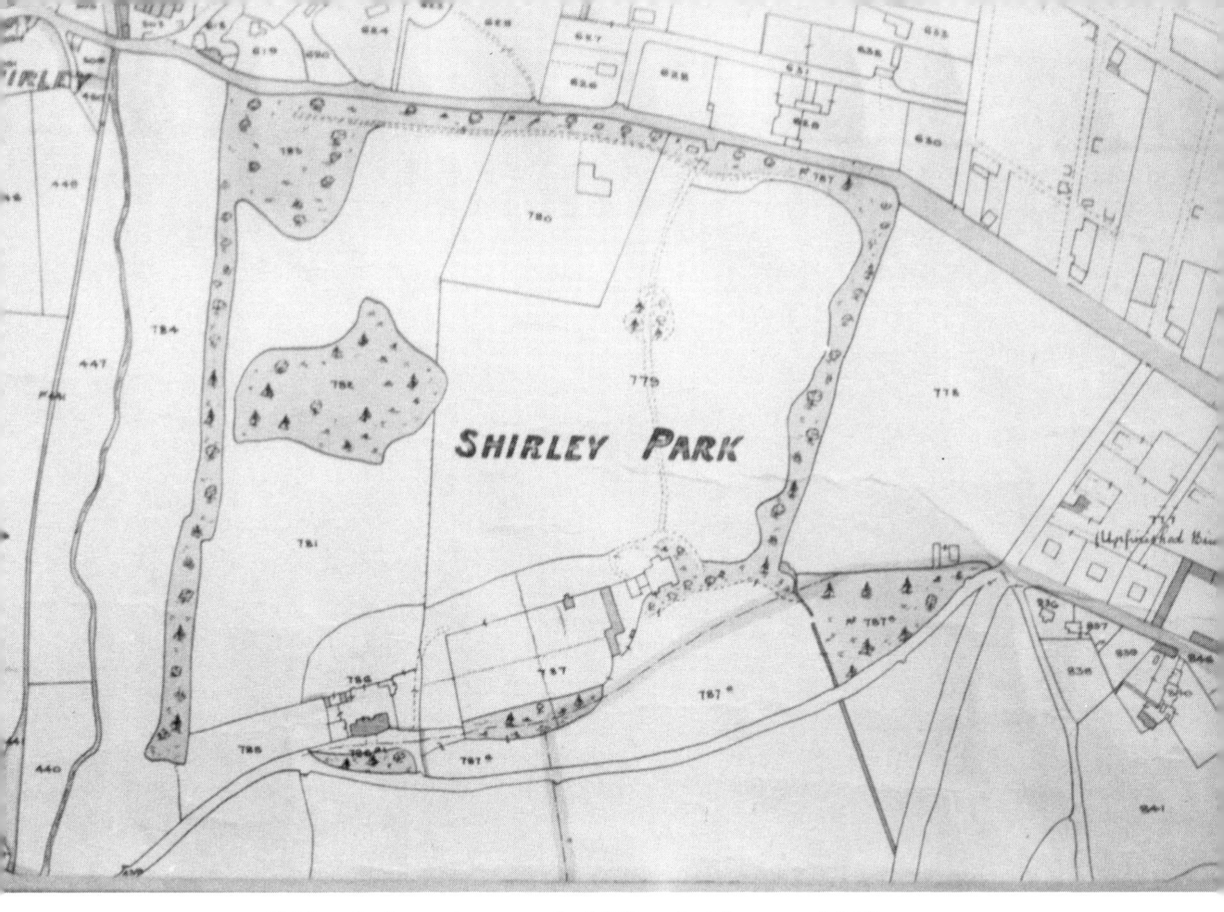

Shirley Park, as shown on the Millbrook tithe map of 1843.
(Courtesy Southampton Record Office).

The Ordnance Survey map of 1865-67 shows the area north from Park Street and across to the line of the future Clarendon Road solidly built up with villas and smaller houses. By this time, Shirley House was occupied only by a caretaker. Mr. Burrows died suddenly, aged 49, in 1859 (his tombstone in the old St. Nicholas cemetery in Millbrook Road is among those recently removed prior to house-building there) and Rev. E. Binney took over running his school but he gave it up after three years: old Shirley House found no further tenants.

The caretaker in 1862-70 was John Webb, who lived there with his family unpaid but rent-free, keeping its many rooms of dust-sheeted furniture in good order and having the right to sell flowers and vegetables grown in the kitchen garden. According to transmitted family memories (communicated by his great-grand-daughter and her nonagenarian aunt), Mr. Webb lost his job when he refused to serve one of the local gentry on a Sunday; he was a Sunday School superintendent who took the Sabbath seriously. Previously, one of his duties had been to keep correct "railway time" for the benefit of neighbouring residents on the big clock over the stable block near Shirley Park Road.

With the house remaining empty, it is not surprising that it was widely believed to be haunted — by the ghost of a young girl whose death was linked with her parents' efforts to prevent her eloping with a stable lad. Mr. Webb's sons found the skeleton of a small baby under the rafters but the local police decided it was too old to warrant criminal investigation. While the Webbs' young children were not frightened, the "haunted" reputation of the old house helped to deter potential tenants, so the building was left to deteriorate. The exact date of its eventual demolition is uncertain but it was evidently before 1886, when flagstones from its old kitchen were re-used for the wash-house floor of at least one newly-built house in Heysham Road.

Meanwhile, W. H. Roe, whose interest had been in the piecemeal development of Shirley Park with smaller-scale houses, had died in 1872, aged 80. Reporting that many braved the October rain to attend his funeral in the Old Cemetery off Hill Lane, the *Southampton Times* noted that Roe had been a staunch nonconformist, identified with East Street Baptist and Above Bar chapels, and that "by dint of energy and honourable dealing he became possessed of considerable property, which he used in performing deeds of mercy and generosity; and in the hearts and homes of many of the poor his memory will be long revered".

Roe's property passed to his son, Josiah Stidder Roe (1828-1901). He lived in the house biblically styled Mount Beulah — off Romsey Road, somewhat north-west of the road that took its name early in the present century, with grounds (a strip of the old Shirley Park estate) stretching down below it to Mousehole Lane (Oakley Road). Following the death of J. S. Roe, this land passed through several hands; in October 1902 ten acres were acquired, for £5,200, by the Hampshire Land and Building Society.

The Society lost no time in splitting it into 113 building plots, along Richville Road (not yet built up) and newly laid out Beulah Road and King Edward Avenue. It issued a large coloured plan, proudly asserting that "the arterial thoroughfare, to be known as King Edward Avenue, will be without equal in the district, both in form, position and width". No terrace building was allowed, only semi-detached and detached houses, of minimum value £250-£300. On March 18, 1903, at the Philharmonic Rooms in Ogle Road, 58 plots were sold by ballot, with options on the other 55 adjoining them. Individual house building extended over some years — with gravel and brick clay conveniently available for digging on the west of the future Percy Road.

The Mount Beulah land was advertised for residential development as the Alexandra Park Estate, taking the name of the long-established girls' private school occupying premises adapted and enlarged from the early Victorian house standing west of the junction of present Richville and Oakley Roads. Originally called Rockhampton (or Roehampton?) House, it was marked on the 1867 OS map as Shirley College, changing to Alexandra College in 1872 when Miss

SHIRLEY HOUSE, within 2 miles of SOUTHAMPTON.

FREEHOLD AND TITHE FREE.

THE ABOVE BEAUTIFUL RESIDENCE

Is to be Let or Sold,

And is most respectfully submitted, by Mr. ROE, to the attention of Ladies and Gentlemen, as

A COMMODIOUS, HEALTHY, AND ECONOMICAL ABODE.

IT CONSISTS

ON THE GROUND FLOOR—Of Inner and Outer Hall,—Noble Staircase,—Two Spacious Drawing Rooms,—with Breakfast and Dining Rooms.

ON THE SECOND FLOOR—Of Boudoir,—Seven Handsome Bed Rooms,—and Secondary Staircase.

ON THE THIRD FLOOR—Of Eight Spacious and Airy Bed Rooms.

IN THE BASEMENT—Of Ample Cellarage and Sundry Apartments.

External of the House are Servants' Offices, Stabling, and Coach Houses.

Attached are Kitchen Gardens, Orchard, and Flower Garden.

THE ESTATE

consists of 45 Acres, part Dairy Farm; but the HOUSE may be possessed with 3, 5, or other number of Acres, not exceeding 45.

The Water is excellent,—the Air Salubrious,—the Soil dry.

Further Particulars may be obtained of the Proprietor, Mr. W. H. ROE, SOUTHAMPTON, who is enabled to offer the Residence on advantageous Terms.

Emma Sherratt took a £90 p.a. lease of the 1¼ acre property. She transferred to it the "ladies' boarding school" she had opened in 1863 at Totton (where the Congregational minister Rev. John Sherratt was probably her father) and named in compliment to the Princess of Denmark who that year came to England to marry the Prince of Wales.

In 1878 Miss Sherratt bought the freehold of the Shirley school from J. S. Roe for £1,400. On her marriage in 1887 to Timothy Horsford of Clapham ("a gentleman of no occupation"), she effected a "deed of partnership for carrying on the profession or business of a Ladies' School" with Amy Maude Mayoss, a former pupil who was already assisting her, and her sister Blanche Ellen — daughters of William Mayoss, "wine merchant, family grocer and tea dealer, High Street, Shirley". The Misses Mayoss lived at the college, running it under the style of "Sherratt and Mayoss" until 1897, when Mrs. Horsford sold her interest for £2,300 and they became joint owners. Amy had by then married Frederick Barnes, a London oil merchant.

Until her death in 1913, aged 87, Mrs. Horsford kept in touch with the school she had founded. It evidently flourished with about thirty boarders — mostly daughters of parents working in the then far-flung British Empire — and twice as many day girls, along with a few little boys. To provide a playing field, the proprietors bought in 1903 from the Hampshire Land and Building Society ten house plots adjoining the school, along the east side of King Edward Avenue. In Edwardian times Alexandra College was advertised as "High School for Girls and Preparatory School for Little Boys: Principals Mrs. Barnes and Miss Mayoss, assisted by certificated and fully qualified staff. Large house and garden; separate classrooms; thorough modern education; preparation for local university examinations. Good playgrounds and games field attached. Hockey, tennis, croquet etc. Fees inclusive of music — boarders from 10 guineas, day pupils from 2 guineas per term".

Highlighting the 50th annual prize distribution in 1913 was a jubilee message of good wishes from Queen Alexandra. The last gathering at the college was in July 1921, when former pupils came to bid farewell to the retiring principals. They sold their 2 acre site and buildings for £4,500 to the local education authority, which incorporated them into its Regents Park Schools, built in 1913 on land immediately north of Alexandra College. Part of its old buildings were demolished in 1954, the rest a decade later.

The naming of Regents Park gave an aura of fashionable elegance to the area where a succession of what the guide books called "handsome suburban residences" or "villas of very neat design" were erected from the 1840s — so whatever their style of architecture, they were actually early Victorian rather than Regency. They were mostly sited in sizeable grounds, approached from the "gracefully winding road" featured in the engraving Philip Brannon included in his "Picture of Southampton" (1850). This may have somewhat

Alexandra College, Shirley, from an Edwardian postcard.

romanticised the view of the "gently ascending land" about which he enthused in his later "Stranger's Guide to Southampton" — "the site is admirable, the aspect warm, the surrounding country varied and rural and the prospect extensive and full of interest".

Some of these Regents Park villas have their names perpetuated by the roads of more modest houses built over their grounds — Clifton Road from about 1900 and Claremont Crescent and Road and Landsowne Road from 1925-30. Stanton Road, dating from 1924, was named after the man who lived at "Newlands" for nearly thirty years from 1880, followed by his widow remaining there until 1920, after which the property was sold for redevelopment. Thomas Harrison Stanton was a solicitor, partner in the firm of Coxwell, Bassett and Stanton, later Stanton, Bassett and Stanton, with offices in Gloucester Square, also at Totton and Lyndhurst.

Regents Park was genteel and secluded but its "carriage folk" of mid-Victorian times cannot have been entirely insulated from workaday activities centred on Tanners Brook, particularly when winds carried odours of the process for which it was named or a reminder of the unsocial intrusion later in the century of a tallow works on a former brickfield, about the middle of today's South Mill Road, not far west of Claremont House.

In his "Companion in a Tour round Southampton" John Bullar wrote in 1809 that "the process of tanning has long been extensively carried on at Millbrook, the neighbouring forest supplying abundance of oak bark and a rapid stream affording the necessary aid of water". As a domestic industry it must have been long established, becoming concentrated on a commercial scale along the lower part of the stream, to which it gave the name of Tanners Brook — probably in the 17th or 18th century, supplanting its earlier designation as Mill Brook, which was applied to the area flanking it.

This was probably the "grindan broc" featuring in a Nursling land charter of 877: "grinding brook" suggests it was already harnessed for corn milling, although the reference may have been to the way it cut its passage through the landscape. "Melebroc" was mentioned in land grants of 956 and 1045 — when King Edward granted it to the Bishops of Winchester, recorded in Doomsday Book as holding it, with 28 villagers. It afterwards belonged to St. Swithun's Priory, until the Reformation, after which Henry VIII settled it on John Mill. Origins of place names are notoriously uncertain but Shirley may derive from Old English words indicating a clearing in woodland or a place of bright water — perhaps the stretch of ponds serving the mill at "Sirelei" listed in the Norman survey of 1086.

The master tanner at Millbrook from about 1810 was John Bridger, evidently a man of some substance, a churchwarden prominent in parish affairs, particularly arrangements for rebuilding and enlarging St. Nicholas church in 1827-28. He had retired by 1843, when the Millbrook tithe map and schedule showed him as owner of the "house, garden, tannery, yard etc." then leased by William Sharland. He later developed other business interests, for the 1859 directory listed him at Redbridge as "shipbuilder, corn and timber merchant etc." Sharland may have been the last of the tanner capitalists of Tanners Brook. The Tanyard House stood on its western bank, just above the point where Millbrook Road crossed it at old Tanners Bridge. After the incorporation of Shirley and Freemantle in 1895, Tanners Brook formed the borough boundary, until the further extension of 1954. Demolished about 1936, Tanyard House was for forty years popularly known as Southampton's "first and last house". In the present century it was occupied by John Knight, following his father of the same name as a vegetable dealer, renting sheds at the old tannery.

Tanneries needed to be located near the outlet of the stream, for it to carry away the noxious wastes involved in the tanning process, while coastal

Regents Park romanticised: an engraving by Philip Brannon, 1850.

breezes helped to disperse the unpleasant smells. Availability of fresh water was an important factor determining patterns of early settlement, while streams provided power for corn mills and later industries — which, even if they did not rely primarily on water power, related their location to the existence of mill buildings suitable for their purposes. In the 19th century manufacturing activity along Tanners Brook was considerable, making it almost a suburban industrial zone, beyond the western fringe of the residential area at Regents Park.

There were three foundries at intervals of less than half a mile along Tanners Brook. Below Shirley and Mousehole was the Vulcan Iron Works, on its east side, opposite the west end of Mill Road, which harks back to earlier activity on the site. Vulcan Road and Close echo the name of the works, where for several years before and after 1860 Charles Kerman was in business as "iron founder, millwright, engineer and miller". He was probably responsible for the building of Vulcan Terrace, a row of a dozen small houses on the north side of Millbrook Road, just east of modern King George's Avenue — originally to accommodate his workmen and their families. This terrace must have contrasted starkly with the spaciously genteel villas nearby.

Vulcan Terrace retained its identity for a hundred years, until demolished in connection with road improvements twenty years ago. Both it and the iron works were shown on the OS map published in 1871 but the 1897 edition marked the former foundry as "varnish works". Still on the map in 1934, but un-named and presumably long disused, the buildings were soon afterwards demolished to make way for new houses in Elmes Drive and Brookside Avenue.

The chief tributary of Tanners Brook is Hollybrook, which rises near Roman Road, Bassett (where a stretch of it forms the city's north-west boundary) and flows down to join the larger stream by the ponds at Old Shirley. The name which now identifies the area to the north-east of Upper Shirley, carried there by Hollybrook Avenue and Road, is of some antiquity, for it was doubtless the "holan broc" i.e. hollow brook, eroding the gravel to create its mini-ravine, mentioned in the North Stoneham land charter of 932.

The wider topographical application of the name of the stream was reinforced by its adoption for the country house built a century and a half ago for Nathaniel Newman Jefferys, who created his Hollybrook House estate on parts of the former Shirley Common and Warren, following their enclosure in 1830. Much of the land was then allotted to the trustees of Gifford Warriner, the lord of the manor, who was declared a lunatic in 1821. With them and their tenants Jefferys engaged in a series of transactions from 1834 (the City Record Office holds boxes of documents for his various leasehold and freehold purchases and mortgages), to assemble a block of 54 acres, north of Winchester Road, between today's Lordswood and Malvern Roads. Hollybrook House itself was sited in a dominating position in the area of modern Linford Crescent.

Hollybrook House in 1838, from a contemporary engraving.
(Courtesy Southampton City Museums).

Deeds dated August 1836 refer to "the mansion house, lodge and cottage lately erected" by Jefferys, with barn, stables etc. "now building". Jefferys then mortgaged his estate, he "having occasion for £3,000". This and other moneys raised over the next six years he applied to more purchases and mortgages, greatly enlarging his lands to the north and west, up to the lines of Dale Valley Road, Warren Avenue, Tremona Road and Coxford Road, to a total of over 200 acres — mostly costing him £22.10s. an acre. They included the future sites of the General Hospital and Hollybrook Cemetery, as well as Clement Hoare's "Vinery" of the 1840s.

N. N. Jefferys (1788-1873) was noted in 1828 as "of Southampton, gentleman" i.e. of independent means. The 1834 directory listed him at Marine Place, Hill. The entry "Major Jeffries, Shirley" in 1836-39 concealed the development of his Hollybrook estate, which must have been related to his marriage at Millbrook parish church on September 23, 1836 to Catherine Bligh, widow of Captain George Bligh of Blighmont House. Jefferys may have been a widower, for the parish register records the burial in 1833 of "Mary Jefferys of Hill".

He probably over-reached himself developing his Hollybrook estate, which in 1837-38 he leased to William Dunne, a successful Southampton merchant. Dunne's intended purchase of it for £5,000 did not materialise, however, and in 1839 he sold to Jefferys the twenty acres between Malvern and Dale Roads. Mr. and Mrs. Jefferys lived at Blighmont for some years, until about 1842 when they re-established themselves at Hollybrook, to spend the rest of their lives there. Jefferys died in 1873, aged 85. His memorial tablet inside the west door of St. James church is flanked by another to his widow, who died at the same age in 1876 — "full of good works and the almsdeeds which she did". Jefferys was also regarded as "a generous friend of the poor".

They were interred in the catacombs of the church with which they had long been closely identified. Jefferys gave the site for St. James church, built in 1836 to serve the growing population of Shirley — then still described as "two miles from Southampton" but increasingly favoured by retired officers and prosperous tradesmen, who had their "neat villas and respectable residences" built along the roads laid out from 1830 across the former Shirley Common. Jefferys also met the cost (£900) of the first "National School" associated with St. James church; in 1867 he donated the site for new and larger church schools in Bellemoor Road and expended £3,000 on the buildings. Enlarged by public subscription in 1873, these were taken over in 1912 by the local authority, which replaced them with the present Shirley schools.

The mortgages effected by Jefferys involved Thomas Knowlys in 1847 and then his widow, Mrs. Anne Maria Martha Knowles. This splendidly named lady lived in some style, with houses at Clifton and Morecambe, and from 1851 was the effective owner of Hollybrook, with Nathaniel and Catherine Jefferys retaining a life interest as occupiers and annuitants.

From 1876 the tenant of Hollybrook for nearly twenty years was Alfred Seymour. Little else is now known of him but, unlike Jefferys, his name is perpetuated by a local street. Seymour Road was laid out by 1898 but not until 1915 were the first two houses (styled Hillsborough and Sledmere) erected there. Others were built from 1925 onwards, complemented in the 1950s by flats in adjoining Seymour Close.

Mrs. Knowlys died early in 1886 — described by Southampton papers as "a considerable landed proprietor", living in retirement and noted for her benevolence. In April that year a score of building plots along Winchester Road and the south side of Chilworth Road (renamed Tremona Road in 1931) were put up for auction at the Royal Hotel, Above Bar. The London agents quaintly presented them as "adjoining Shirley, which is a rising watering place, with good sea bathing, and owing to its situation and the dry character of

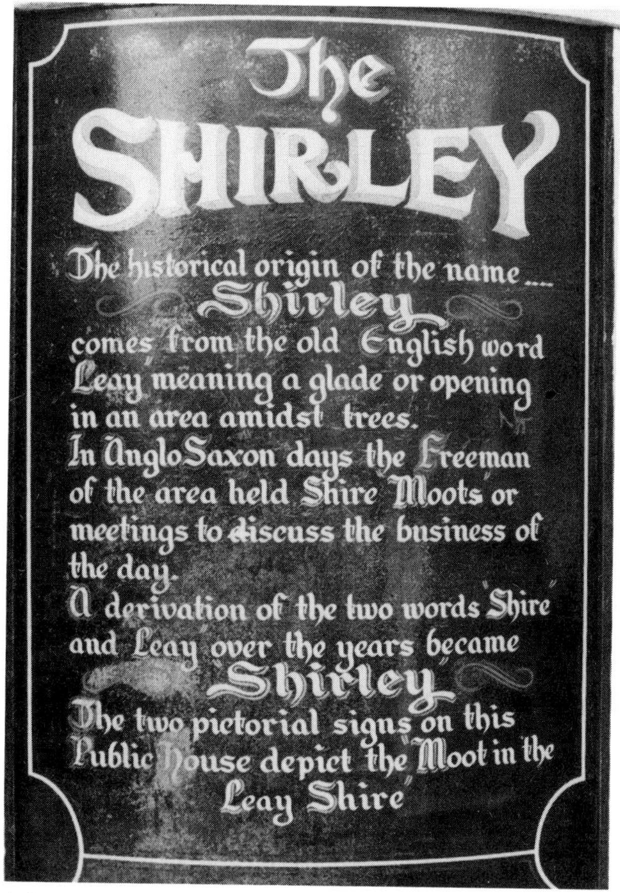

The origin of the name Shirley as given at "The Shirley" public house. (Photograph: Tom Holder).

the soil the climate is particularly healthy and exhilarating". Further housing development followed after a Southampton solicitor, Herbert Blatch, bought 126 acres of the Hollybrook estate for £12,800.

In 1902 the corporation bought from him 47 acres north of the stream and after extinguishing the tenancy of John Jenman of Hollybrook Farm laid it out as a new cemetery, opened in 1913. In 1910 the Board of Guardians acquired the "fine old residence" and a strip of 13 acres, extending from Lordswood Road to the present Hollybrook Avenue. It cost them £3,150 and they spent nearly as much adapting the house as a home for "pauper boys" — opened in August 1912, with a large garden party, at which local notables were entertained by the boys' drum and fife band. In 1914 the corporation bought 11 acres to the south (Hollybrook Farm) from the builder John Smith of Avenue House, with the intention of erecting "working class dwellings" but five years later it transferred this land to the Guardians, who built new "cottage homes" to take the girls moved to Hollybrook from the "Poor Law Institution" in St. Mary Street.

After the Education Committee took over the Children's Home (as the Hollybrook premises were then called) in 1930, it added more cottage homes and made other additions, including a nursery and staff accommodation. In 1955 the complex was closed, the children being dispersed into smaller units and families. The pre-war staff wing was incorporated in 1958 into a new primary school, remodelled in 1970 as Hollybrook Middle School. Hollybrook House itself was demolished about 1950 and the grounds were used for housing, including adaptations of the cottage homes. One is now styled Seymour House, another continues the name of Hollybrook House — now the Trading Standards Office. The entrance lodge of the original Hollybrook House on Winchester Road disappeared in 1978 but the gateway and part of the former carriage drive to the "big house" still survive beside Seymour Road.

To the west, Vinery Road and Vinery Gardens, dating respectively from about 1900 and 1920, recall another vanished "country house" which stood above the northern bank of the Hollybrook stream for nearly a century, until demolished in 1938 for the building of new houses along Tremona Road. For most of that time Hoare's Hill carried the name of the man for whom "The Vinery" was built soon after 1840 but in 1924 the borough council decided to change it to Dale Road — presumably in response to representations that the old name did not suit a modern residential road. Whatever its social disadvantages in spoken usage, one may now regret the disappearance of this topographical association with Clement Hoare's adjoining vineyard of the 1840s.

Probably the only English vine-grower to receive recognition as such in the august pages of the *Dictionary of National Biography*, Hoare had cultivated a vineyard at Sidlesham, near Chichester, before moving to Southampton about 1840. In 1843 he was recorded as occupying over 100 acres, mostly leased from N. N. Jefferys, lying north of Winchester Road between the present Dale Road and Warren Avenue. Before Hoare's name became attached to it, the road abutting this land was known as Camp Road, leading to the area where troops encamped for embarkation to the European wars of the 18th and 19th centuries. The Southampton directories of 1843-45 listed him at "Vine House", Shirley Common or Warren, first as "cultivator of the vine", then more grandly as "vigneron" — although he grew grapes for eating rather than wine-making. Hoare was a specialist grower and writer; in 1835 he published *A Practical Treatise on the Cultivation of the Grape on Open Walls*, which went through three editions in six years.

Opposite: Hollybrook House in 1912 as a home for "pauper boys" - with their fife and drum band. (Courtesy Southampton Central Library).

He established himself "at Shirley, about two miles from Southampton" with a good eye to the terrain, quickly developing his vineyard on the northern slope of Hollybrook — land now allotment gardens. Hoare had his "villa" built above it, opposite Laundry Road, approached by what was formerly Chilworth Road. To end confusion with its counterpart in Bassett, this was renamed Tremona Road in 1933, taking the name of another early Victorian house to the west of Hoare's — Tre Mona Court, which between the wars accommodated the "Southampton Seamen's Orphanage for Boys" and later part of the School of Radiography of the nearby General Hospital.

Hoare was visited in 1843 by J. C. Loudon, "Conductor" of the *Gardeners' Magazine,* who came to Southampton to help the Corporation plan its new cemetery on the Common. He wrote a perceptive set of "hints for the improvement of the town", including far-sighted comments on such matters as sanitation, sewerage, street layout and reclamation of the mudlands. Loudon was scathing about local architecture: "We have seldom seen a town where so many buildings have recently been erected and so very little taste exhibited in them. With the exception of the railway station and the villa of Mr. Hoare at Shirley, we cannot refer to one specimen of good taste." Vine House, designed by a Mr. Elliott of Chichester, he thought "a gem of beauty".

Loudon described Hoare's methods of growing vines on previously barren heath and gravel, against low brick walls, around hollow columns and also under glass, applying his principles of "concentration of sap" and limited grape yield. Loudon noted that "on the opposite bank Mr. Hoare has planted a pine wood, which has already an excellent effect, besides its utility in shutting out the rising village". In 1844 Hoare published "a descriptive account of an improved method of planting and managing the roots of grape vines", based on his experience at Shirley Warren. He was not listed there in 1847, so must have left by then, perhaps owing to ill-health: he died at Vauxhall, Surrey in 1849, aged 60.

After the vineyard was given up, the house — styled "The Vinery" for the rest of its existence — became the residence of "persons of substance", like the banker R. C. Hankinson in the 1860s. From 1901 it was occupied by Captain E. M. Manning, then by his widow from 1909 to 1920. In 1922-28 The Vinery was the family home of George Warren, a sea-going marine engineer from Liverpool. His son of the same name has kindly provided recollections of his boyhood years (6-12) happily spent there. The old house was initially completely shrouded in ivy, later removed for structural reasons, to reveal some fine yellow brickwork. Behind the brick wall and decorative iron railings flanking carriage drives off Chilworth/Tremona Road grew many tall trees, with thick rhododendron bushes beneath them. The north aspect of the house was somewhat gloomy but the south and west sides were very pleasant. French windows opened on to grassy banks, leading down to lawns and gardens, with a summer house and tennis court. Mrs. Warren and her

"The Vinery" about 1925. (Courtesy Mrs. I.M. Priestley).

teenage daughter Irene (inevitably nicknamed Shirley) ran a private tennis club, the Chilworth Tennis Party, and held various social events at The Vinery, including fund-raising to provide wireless sets for the nearby Infirmary.

To the west were kitchen gardens and an orchard, while in the south-west corner of the grounds young George and a friend were able to build a tree house. Besides the delights of the stream, the Hollybrook valley afforded fine toboggan slides. East of the house was a dairy farm, tenanted by a family named Dixon. Its pastures surrounded The Vinery's walled grounds, the further parts of which had become very overgrown — all the more attractive to youngsters. The house was spacious, having some twenty rooms, including five large attics for servants, with a separate spiral staircase from the kitchen area — where a bell system had operated to summon attendance throughout the house. There was also a large bell fixed outside, between two chimney stacks; the rope was soon cut off out of a boy's reach! Below the house were extensive cellars, an exciting world for exploration by candlelight; the house itself was still lit only by gas in the Twenties. At its south-west corner was a large conservatory, with some hanging vines surviving from Clement Hoare's day.

After the Warrens removed to a house in Regents Park Road, The Vinery stood empty until 1931, when it was taken by Herbert Miller, followed in 1937 by Arthur Bromby. A year later residential development along Tremona Road was continued across the frontage, involving the demolition of the old house.

In 1948 a local resident complained to the Council about the inconveniences arising through the similarity of the names of Dale Road and Dale Valley Road and suggested that the former should revert to its old designation of Hoare's Hill — but the Works Committee decided to take no action in the matter.

While other residents sometimes seek to change old street names that may be thought outmoded or unflattering, most people seem to develop an affection for them, whatever their origins, and prefer to see them retained. In the case of Laundry Road, the *Southern Evening Echo* unwittingly sparked off a controversy that ran through most of 1966. On January 3, its "Tom Bargate" column referred to Christmas 1965 as the 102nd and last spent by members of the Harrison family in their home at 75 Laundry Road, then about to be demolished for redevelopment with a block of flats. It was a farmhouse, about 120 years old, formerly the centre of Shirley Warren dairy, which the Harrisons took over in 1863: their cows grazed on fields where now stands Southampton General Hospital. The Harrisons began retailing milk in 1880 and established a "model dairy" in Vaudrey Street. They later moved to a farm at Bitterne Park, where their riverside meadows have become sports fields and public open space. Harrisons merged in 1940 with A. Brown's Hill Lane dairy; the business became part of South Coast Dairies in 1957.

Laundry Road was so called because of the number of laundresses working at their cottages there in Victorian times. The name must have been in local use for some decades before it was noted on maps and in directory lists towards the end of the last century, when the road was built up with more houses. Taking in washing was a respectable Victorian occupation, especially for widows who then had few opportunities of earning money to maintain themselves and their families, but in 1966 references to the humble origins of Laundry Road offended some residents. They protested to the *Echo* and organised a petition to the City Council requesting its name be changed.

Signed by 120 people representing 68 out of 102 households, the petition claimed their road name carried a stigma; the residents were being socially pilloried and their house values reduced. On February 4, the Public Works Committee responded by resolving "that Laundry Road be re-named St. Jude's Road as suggested by the petitioners". When it met on April 1, however, it heard that another petition had been received, protesting against the change. The committee therefore rescinded its previous decision "because of the

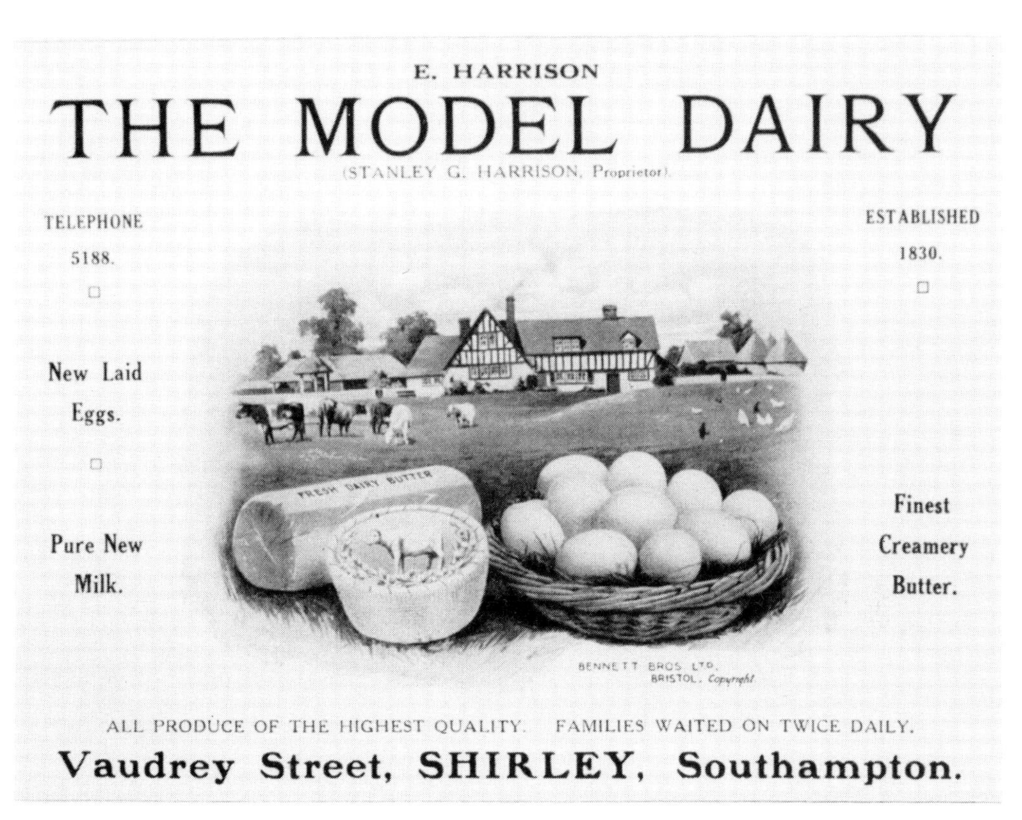

An advertisement in Southampton's Official Guide of 1931.

divergence of views among the householders". It was noticed that some people had signed both petitions!

The Coxford Labour Party then took up the vexed question and asked that a referendum be held. The council agreed and the Town Clerk sent out 120 letters asking "Do you wish the name of Laundry Road to be changed to St. Jude's Road?" In September, he reported 80 replies — 56 wanting no change and only 24 favouring re-naming. A month later the Council confirmed its committee's decision "that the name of Laundry Road be not changed".

Between the sites of Hollybrook House and The Vinery, Bladon Road recalls another vanished house, a more modest yellow brick villa, with coach house and stables, which occupied a site of about an acre, almost opposite the top of Wilton Road. For the last 36 years of his long life, Bladon Lodge was the home of the distinguished Hampshire painter, William Shayer — who is also commemorated by Shayer Road, on the south side of Winchester Road.

Both roads were laid out from about 1900, some twenty years after Shayer's burial in the churchyard of nearby St. James.

Shayer lived most of his 92 years in his native Southampton. Born in 1787, he was the son the landlord of the "Turk's Head" in Spring Gardens and later the "Horse and Jockey" in East Street — who died in 1792, leaving his widow to manage the inn and bring up a young family. William began work assisting a painter of ornamental furniture, then served an apprenticeship as a coach painter and heraldic artist. His work took him to Guildford, then in 1810 to Chichester, where he married his master's niece, Sarah Earle, and remained for nearly ten years. The craft of coach painting involved painstaking and intricate work, providing the basis on which many provincial artists of the period developed their wider talents.

From decorations and funeral hatchments, Shayer steadily extended his painting, particularly after his return to Southampton in 1819. He attracted the attention of Michael Hoy, a rich merchant with estates at Midanbury, Thornhill and on the Isle of Wight (see *Streets*, page 102); it was noted in 1827 that Hoy "with the munificence of a true patron of art employed Mr. Shayer until his rooms were almost covered with his works and thus gave this native artist the means and heart to prosecute his toilsome way".

Shayer first exhibited at the Royal Academy in 1820. He was then living in French Street, next to the theatre, for which he probably painted scenery, as well as augmenting his income by giving drawing lessons. Shayer's connection with the theatre — which introduced gas lighting in 1822 — influenced his later style, for many of his paintings have a theatrical atmosphere, with a low dramatic light concentrated on the principal figures.

Shayer lost his first wife in 1823 but soon afterwards married another, Elizabeth Waller. Living until 1866, she also lies buried in St. James churchyard, together with two of her sons, Henry and Charles, who, like their father's eldest son, William, also became professional painters. Shayer had five children by each of his wives and the pressure to support them in their early years must have provided incentive for his increasing output at the easel. In 1827 a reviewer in the *Southampton Herald* wrote "when we remember that this artist has worked his own way from obscurity to eminence and has, by his industry, brought up most respectably a numerous family, we feel for him severe respect and trust that for the honour of his native place such true talent and unremitting assiduity will meet with proper patronage and due reward . . . We fully understand how great the struggle must have been for him to rise to the height he has done with a numerous family, and his perseverance does him honour."

In 1828, Shayer moved to 158 High Street, next door to the Hampshire Picture Gallery opened the previous year by Henry Buchan, which gave more opportunities for local display and sale of Shayer's increasingly acclaimed work.

William Shayer (1787-1879) and (below) Bladon Lodge – his home for his last 36 years.

Five years later he took a house at 10 Hanover Buildings, where he lived for ten years before briefly removing to Nursling and then establishing himself in 1843 at his semi-rural villa off Winchester Road. He called it Bladon Lodge in compliment to his wife's mother, Mary Bladon.

Shayer declined invitations to set himself up in the London art world. He was content to remain in Southampton, although thereby losing some of the greater recognition he might have gained during his lifetime and being obliged to produce perhaps too many paintings for sale at modest prices: he received only guineas for pictures which now fetch thousands of pounds. From the 1840s Shayer increased his already considerable output through a studio "production line" with the help of his sons — he adding the figures and details to their backgrounds and also collaborating with other artists on the same basis. He painted pairs and sequences of subjects essentially the same but with enough minor variations to merit different titles.

He found his main inspiration and material in and around the New Forest, painting woodland glades, gypsy camps, groups of country folk and animals, rural and coastal scenes — sometimes idealised but generally authentically "picturesque" and not excessively sentimentalised. Executed in a distinctive style, finely detailed and full of local and period charm, Shayer's work is increasingly esteemed and represented in many collections, including Southampton Art Gallery. An authoritative account is given by Brian Stewart and Mervyn Cutting in their book "The Shayer Family of Painters" (1981).

Bladon Lodge would have disappeared sooner if plans for the Didcot, Newbury and Southampton Railway had materialised. Plans of 1883 showed its line running down from Chilworth, slicing through the site of Shayer's old home and then under Winchester Road to Shirley, where there would have been a station near St. James church; along the west of Wilton Road and under Hill Lane by Archers Road, through the Dell (earmarked for a goods yard) and along an embankment between Hill Lane and the Polygon, across a viaduct over Commercial Road and the LSWR line, on to reclaimed mudland and a station at the west end of Bargate Street. The DNSR acquired property along this route and started construction work (some traces of the embankment still survive west of the Polygon) but it over-reached itself and had to suspend its Southampton preparations in October 1883. After the opening of the line from Newbury to Winchester in 1885 the company was obliged to settle for a junction with the LSWR at Shawford, completed in 1891.

For twenty years from 1883 Shirley had its Station Road but no station: in 1903 the Corporation changed its misleading name to Stratton Road. The reason for this choice remains obscure: the surname Stratton was not unknown in Shirley but no-one is now identifiable as prominent enough to merit having a road called after him. Didcot and Newbury Roads still carry echoes of the abortive railway scheme — already suspended when they were laid out in 1887 and abandoned before they were built up in the early 1890s.

Beyond Stratton Road, the names of Hyde Close, Ridding Close and Vaudrey Close are noteworthy as three of the few instances of women memorialised on the Southampton street scene. Vaudrey Close continues the name of the older Vaudrey Street, which was itself a redesignation of the original Bevois Street, changed by the Corporation in 1901 to end its duplication after Shirley was incorporated into the borough in 1895. It was adopted in compliment to Mrs. Marianne Vaudrey, who assumed the name Barker-Mill in 1903, having previously inherited the extensive family estates that made her lady of several manors, including parts of Shirley.

Redevelopment of the Church Street area from 1960 gave occasion for the Vaudrey association to be complemented by Hyde and Ridding, taking the names of two ladies who lived there in the 1840s, before it was built up with terraces of small Victorian houses that a century later were themselves subject to clearance. The 1843 Millbrook tithe map showed Dorothy Hyde living in the neighbourhood, at a villa with four acres of "lawn": another resident was Miss Ridding, daughter of the former Town Clerk of Southampton, Thomas Ridding.

His father of the same name was Town Clerk from 1787 until his death in 1804. His son held the same office from 1810 until retiring in 1838. He is remembered for having secured from the corporation in 1814 a long lease on the former town brickyard, an acre and a half "situated in and surrounded by Southampton Common, west of the Southampton Arms where the cowherd dwelleth", on which was erected for him a fashionable five-bedroom Georgian "cottage". Following Ridding's death in 1844 his widow's trustees assigned "Hawthorn Cottage" in 1851 to the Northam shipbuilder John Ransom, a colourful character who lived there until his death in 1886. The house was then taken by James Newman, whose widow remained there until 1942. After her death, her daughters sold their interest in 1945 to the Corporation, which demolished the house, then dilapidated after war-time damage. The grounds were used as a tree nursery until leased in 1961 to J. Chipperfield for a "zoological pets corner" — given up in 1984.

The lady commemorated by Vaudrey Street/Close had inherited the Eling estates of her father Frederick Ibbotson, who died in 1871. Sixteen years later she became the sole owner of the much larger Barker-Mill lands, including parts of Shirley, Millbrook, Redbridge, Nursling and Rownhams, Mottisfont, Longstock and Langley; she also owned considerable estates at King's Somborne and on the fringes of the New Forest, at Colbury and Marchwood. Most of these lands were held in the 18th century by the Mill family — whose arms are among those adorning the north face of the Bargate. When Sir Charles Mill, the tenth baronet, died in 1835, he left his property to his sister's son, Rev. John Barker, who assumed the arms and name of Mill and was himself made a baronet the following year. On his death in 1860, without issue, the family estates went to his widow, Jane, and when she died in 1884 they passed to Mrs. Vaudrey.

She was a third cousin of Sir John Barker-Mill and a descendant of William, Lord Sandys, Lord Chamberlain to Henry VIII. Following its dissolution in 1536, Mottisfont Priory had been granted to him by the King — in exchange for the then villages of Chelsea and Paddington!

Marianne Ibbotson, of Langley Manor, Colbury, had married a Liverpool solicitor, William Vaudrey, in 1872 at fashionable St. George's, Hanover Square. He died in 1887, whereupon she became sole owner of the Barker-Mill estates. Apart from the years 1900-14 spent at Mottisfont, she lived at Langley Manor until her death in 1932, aged 86. Between 1885 and 1900 Mottisfont was leased to a London businessman of Danish-German extraction, Daniel Meinhertzhagen. His son Richard gave his recollections of those years in his book *Diary of a Black Sheep*, published in 1964, in which he wrote: "The story goes that Sir John Barker-Mill left Mottisfont and considerable land at Stockbridge and Southampton to his next of kin without knowing the identity of his heir. His lawyer was a north countryman called Vaudrey, who ferreted out the heir, a distant relative, a most unattractive girl, and married her and did not disclose her prospects until Sir John died." Whatever the truth of this story, Vaudrey had only three years to share his wife's riches: she outlived him by another 45 years, devoting herself to managing her estates and exercising her influence in the Test Valley and New Forest areas in various benevolent ways.

She was a generous supporter of church and Sunday schools, youth, sports and charity organisations, as well as being a discreet benefactress of many people on her estates. The village hall at Colbury was built as a memorial to the eldest of her four sons and other men of the area killed in World War I. She was a strong temperance advocate and took opportunities to close several licensed premises on her property. Disapproving of horse racing — perhaps because one of her sons had run up heavy debts at Stockbridge — she revoked the lease of part of that racecourse, forcing racing to be transferred to Salisbury.

When she lived at Mottisfont, she spent some £40,000 on renovation work — which revealed significant survivals of the original priory buildings — but refused to countenance central heating or electricity, either there or at Langley Manor. After her return there in 1914, Mottisfont remained largely unoccupied (its contents sold in 1927) until it was purchased from her grandson in 1934 by Gilbert Russell, whose widow gave it to the National Trust in 1957. In her younger days, Mrs. Vaudrey thought little of walking from Langley to Southampton and back but her later years were spent in seclusion, as a somewhat eccentric recluse. She was buried in the family vault at St. Andrew's church, Mottisfont, beside the husband she had so long outlived.

Her gifts included a church site at Maybush and twelve acres to Millbrook parish council for the making of Green Park recreation ground. Meeting on September 28, 1933, the day of George Gover's death, the council discussed placing a drinking fountain there "as a perpetual recognition of his memory" but two months later it resolved that the road from Redbridge to Test Lane, then about to be built up, should be called Gover Road in tribute to the man whose genial personality and long involvement in local affairs had made him a popular and important figure in Millbrook. George Gover, of Bridgers Farm, Wimpson, was a market gardener for most of his 72 years. He joined the parish council in 1895, the year after its creation, and continued a member for 38 years, serving as chairman in 1913-24 and 1926-31. Elmes Drive by Tanners Brook, developed around 1938, was likewise given the name of another Millbrook councillor, George Elmes, J.P. He served on the parish council in 1922-24 and 1931-47 and was its chairman in 1937-40. From 1932 he also represented Millbrook on the District Council.

The first of the three Millbrook councillors accorded road name honour by their parish colleagues in the Thirties was Owen Llewellyn Mansel, who died in 1931, aged 67. He spent the latter part of his life in Millbrook, having earlier lived east of the Itchen. Son of a former Dorset vicar and a cousin of Lord Radstock of Mayfield House, Mansel was a bachelor able to enjoy varied interests. His hobbies included breeding prize-winning Labrador dogs but he devoted much of his time and energy to public service, notably for the N.S.P.C.C. and as a local councillor, first on the old Itchen Urban District Council, then at Millbrook.

He made his home at the old Manor House, which in the 1920s was run as a select boarding house by Miss F. M. Bond. Standing opposite Holy Trinity church, it was demolished in 1947. Its site lies under the westbound carriageway of today's Millbrook Road, while its grounds were taken for factory development, in the area appropriately named Manor House Avenue in 1961. Thirty years previously, the former country lane between Wimpson and Upper Wimpson Farms — which seems to have existed for many years without an "official" name — was designated Mansel Road. It now has a dual existence, divided into two sections, styled East and West, separated by Mansel Park, at the heart of the large post-war housing estate.

For most of the years 1919-30 O.L. Mansel was an active member of the parish council and of the South Stoneham Rural District Council and Board of Guardians, successively chairman of both these bodies in 1923-25. "He laboured strenuously in the interests of the parish and accomplished a great deal of good work" was George Gover's tribute in 1931. An example was his successful campaign to get the first allocation of council houses built at Wimpson in 1926: he vigorously rebutted economy-minded arguments that old cottages would still serve if repaired and got them condemned as "not decent for the twentieth century". In the last year of his life, Mansel was still

The old Millbrook church of St. Nicholas, long disused but not demolished until 1939 (from a postcard issued about 1922 by George Ayles, of Testwood Road Post Office).

championing Millbrook interests, pressing for better facilities at Wimpson and Redbridge schools, of which he was a manager, and being ready to go on a deputation to London only a few weeks before he died.

Mansel also urged that Millbrook should join Southampton, rather than be switched to Romsey and Stockbridge District Council — as happened in 1932 when the old South Stoneham district was extinguished. In 1930 he got his resolution on joining the borough carried unanimously at a special parish meeting but at that time Southampton missed the opportunity to take in Millbrook, which was not incorporated until 1954, in very different circumstances.

Freemantle and Foundry Lane

At Freemantle, Sir George's Road and Hewitt's Road combine to commemorate the former owner of the country house estate, recalled by Mansion Road and Park Road, that stretched between Millbrook and Shirley Roads, until built over in mid-Victorian times to become a suburb of Southampton — into which it was incorporated by the boundary extension of 1895. Payne's Road memorialises the property developer who initiated this transformation by buying all 143 acres in 1852, demolishing old Freemantle House and laying out a score of roads across its site and parkland.

But what of the name Freemantle itself? The elegant country mansion that gave way to smaller Victorian houses was a Georgian replacement of an older farm house with a much longer but sketchily documented history. The earliest known owner of "land in Mullebroke called Fremantel" was William Ace, in the second quarter of the 14th century. Two centuries later, the Corporation's "Book of Remembrance" recorded that on his death in 1558 a Southampton merchant, Thomas Fasshon, left " a house called Free Mantell in the parish of Millbrook, with lands belonging to it" to his eldest son of the same name — who was not to sell the property without the permission of the mayor and aldermen. The elder Fasshon, who was blessed with five sons and seven daughters by his two wives, was mayor of Southampton in 1545 and one of its two M.P.s in 1555. He died a resident of London, having evidently prospered, so the Freemantle estate may have been his "country seat" as well as a farmstead.

The origins and meanings of old place names are often obscure and clouded by supposition. One can only speculate whether Freemantle originated locally or was somehow adopted from its counterpart in Kingsclere, where it is noted under variant spellings from 1180 onwards, including the Latin version Frigidum Mantell in 1214. Freemantle might initially have been both a personal and a place name; its persistence could result from the name of an early owner becoming attached to the land — as happened with the Banastre family at Banister Court (see *Streets*, page 9; also pages 65-66 for the association of the name Freemantle with part of old Bitterne Common early in the last century). Surnames often derived from nicknames, sometimes related to a person's dress, job or status. The Victorian authority on surnames, C.W. Bardsley, suggested that Freemantle "probably owed its origin to the friese cloth which the Frieslanders of the Low Countries once manufactured out of our own wool". According to the current "Oxford Dictionary of English Place Names" (E. Ekwall), "The name is borrowed from France, where Fromentel is a common name. Freemantle is the name of a forest. The name means 'cold cloak'. It may be explained by the Swedish saying that 'the forest is the poor man's jacket'. The forest at best would be a cold jacket".

A forest connection would fit this part of Hampshire, near the New Forest. While it must remain uncertain how it came to be used, personalised and attached to the land and house, it would seem likely that Freemantle indeed stems from the old French words meaning "cold cloak"; perhaps they were once applied in contemptuous reference to an ill-dressed man or one living in a poor house affording little shelter? Maybe Freemantle was once a sort of "cold comfort farm"!

"Free Mantle Farm" was marked on Isaac Taylor's Hampshire map of 1759. J. Linden's "Southampton Guide" of 1768 (the first of its kind, reflecting the growth of the town as a spa and fashionable resort) gave a flowery account of the house and grounds being created at Bellevue for Nathaniel St. André but made no mention of Freemantle — which suggests that it had not then been developed from a farmhouse into a "gentleman's residence". Its enhanced status was noted in the 1775 edition of Baker's "Southampton Guide", which described Freemantle as "the seat of James Amyatt Esq., a pretty situation well sheltered with trees; there is a good garden, hot houses and shrubberies".

James Amyatt (1734-1813) came of a family prominent in the affairs of Totnes, where his father was mayor in 1739. In 1754 he enlisted the support of Charles Taylor, who wrote to his brother-in-law Admiral Edward Vernon asking him to get "a place in the India service or in a merchant ship" for his friend Amyatt, who "was esteemed a very sober young man and a good seaman". Influence and patronage may have assisted Amyatt's advancement to a captaincy with the East India Company, which allowed him to trade on his own account. In twenty years he acquired the means to retire and secure election in 1774 as M.P. for Totnes, then a "pocket borough" where considerable "sweetening" of voters must have been needed to succeed. Amyatt's six year term in Parliament was unremarkable; there is no record of him ever addressing the House, although then, as later, his membership and support of the government doubtless brought rewards after the fashion of the time.

Having established himself at Freemantle, Amyatt did not seek re-election at Totnes in 1780 but in 1784 he successfully put himself forward as a candidate at Southampton. He was returned as one of the borough's two M.P.s at the subsequent elections of 1790, 1796, 1802 and 1806 but retired before the 1807 election. Although never prominent at Westminster, where he spoke but rarely, Amyatt evidently satisfied his Southampton constituents and must have contributed to advancing the town's interests during his 22 years' service as their representative. Perhaps he overstrained his finances, because he left the Freemantle estate he must have spent heavily on creating and moved about 1790 to a smaller house near Millbrook. Baker's "Guide" of a decade later, after referring to Freemantle (then described as being "a mile and a half north-west from Southampton"), noted that "a little further on is the fanciful cottage of James Amyatt Esq., M.P. for Southampton, which occupies a delightful spot at the entrance of Millbrook, a pleasant village, with several genteel houses extending nearly to Redbridge".

T. Milne's map of 1791 marked Freemantle as occupied by John Jarrett. Initially a tenant, he bought the freehold from Sir Charles Mill in 1798 for £3,000. Contemporary maps are not of large enough scale to indicate the exact boundaries of the estate but one of 1802, surveyed by John Doswell and Son of Romsey, suggests that Jarrett had enlarged it, not only to the area it comprised at the time of its sale fifty years later but also to include a triangular block west of Foundry Lane, which must have been separated earlier, probably after Jarrett's death in 1809.

His background remains obscure but he was evidently a man of wealth, some of which was expended on "improvements" at Freemantle to suit his taste. The 1804 edition of Baker's guidebook noted that "some of the apartments are sumptuously elegant", while in their "Beauties of England and Wales" published the same year, Britton and Brayley wrote of "the villa of John Jarrett Esq., the interior of which is very elegantly ornamented and particularly a parlour whose sides are veneered with choice marble, purchased in Italy by the present proprietor. The library and drawing room are tastefully ornamented with arabesque paintings. Two neat lodges have lately been erected with artificial stone". A later account by G.F. Prosser in his "Select Illustrations of Hampshire" (1833) described the house as "a plain stuccoed quadrangular building of three fronts": this belied its lavish interior — "the entrance hall is ornamented with marble columns, beyond which is a handsome stone staircase, the walls of the landing being decorated with moulded enrichments. The drawing room is ornamented with an elegant statuary marble chimney-piece, brought from Italy by Mr. Jarrett. The dining room, thirty-two by twenty-one feet, has its walls lined entirely with Italian marble (which Mr. Jarrett effected at very considerable cost) and contains a massive side-board of verd antique".

On Jarrett's death, Freemantle passed to his brother and uncle, both sharing the name Herbert Newton Jarrett; they sold the estate in 1810 to John Hill. He had only a few years to enjoy his purchase before dying early in 1814, at the age of 62. His burial is recorded in the parish register of the old Millbrook church of St. Nicholas (which stood on the south side of Millbrook Road, opposite Regents Park Road; it was superseded by Holy Trinity, consecrated in 1874, but continued as a chapel of ease for some decades, although disused and decaying when finally demolished in 1939). Hill's son and heir, Henry Hill, seems to have continued living at Freemantle, although in 1817 he sold or mortgaged the estate to Josias Dupré Alexander and James Dupré. Five years later, by conveyance dated October 15, 1822, the property was bought by General Sir George Hewett, in whose family it remained until sold in 1852 as building land.

Deeds and schedules of title in Southampton Record Office, from which these details are drawn, make it clear that Freemantle was never owned by the celebrated actress Sarah Siddons. No mention of her having occupied Freemantle, even on a brief tenancy, can be found in the pages of her several biographers or in contemporary sources — apart from the questionable passing reference of 1816, first published in 1961, which has been taken up and embroidered by some recent writers. In his anthology *Southampton: Visitors' Descriptions*, R. Douch included an excerpt from an anonymous manuscript held in the British Museum, a personal "journal of a tour from Brighton to Weymouth in 1816". Recording a drive from Southampton to Lyndhurst, the writer mentioned Freemantle as "a very fine park on your right hand lately sold by Mrs. Siddons". He cannot be regarded as a reliable chronicler, since he wrote only as a casual visitor, liable to misunderstand what he heard; thus he linked a stagnant ditch with the ill-fated canal, intended to connect Southampton with Basingstoke rather than Salisbury. If not simply misinformed about Mrs. Siddons having lately owned Freemantle, perhaps he had a confused recollection of being told about the house in Above Bar that belonged to her in 1812-14.

Dating from about 1758 and the largest of several such town houses (rated at £100, compared with £75 for Ogle House early in the 19th century), it stood at the head of grounds extending westward, below "Caneshot otherwise Windmill Lane" — later restyled Regent Street. Portland Street was laid out across them from 1827. Mrs. Siddons bought the property on September 29, 1812 from Richard Evamy, who ran the nearby Spa Gardens, but sold it back to him for £3,500 on June 24, 1814. Three days later he mortgaged it to her for £3,000 and she held the mortgage until 1824. Although "The Incomparable Sarah" may have envisaged living in Southampton on retiring from the London stage in 1812, it is doubtful if she ever did, certainly not for long. All Saints quarterly rate books marked the house "void" from mid-1812 until 1815, after which it was occupied by others until demolished for redevelopment of its site.

Mrs. Siddons (1755-1831) had a Southampton connection through her most devoted admirer and intimate friend over half a lifetime, Mrs. Charlotte Fitzhugh, wife of William Fitzhugh of Banister Court (see *Streets*, page 9). Mrs. Fitzhugh (1767-1855) was the eldest daughter of Rev. Anthony Hamilton, archdeacon of Colchester and vicar of St. Martin's in the Fields, and sister of William Hamilton, the antiquary and diplomat, secretary to Lord Elgin, who secured the Rosetta Stone from the French and helped collect the famous Grecian marbles. During the London "season", she was a frequent companion and dressing room visitor of the great actress; at other times she maintained an extensive correspondence with her and regularly entertained her at "Bannisters", where the dining room had a place of honour for the portrait of her idol, which she commissioned in 1804 from Thomas Lawrence and presented to the National Gallery in 1843. The Fitzhugh theatrical connection was continued by her daughter Emily and Fanny Kemble, who enjoyed a close but less intensive friendship, lasting long after Banister Court had been sold out of the family in 1858.

If Mrs. Siddons had any connection with Freemantle, it would surely have been mentioned in 19th century guidebooks, which rarely failed to recall an association with the poet Cowper. John Bullar set the pattern when he wrote in his 1809 "Companion" that "this spot will excite interest in many when they recollect that in some of his letters to Lady Hesketh the amiable, pious and melancholy Cowper refers to days of his early life spent at Freemantle, in the enjoyment of that unclouded sunshine of the breast which is the peculiar privilege of the morning of life". Subsequent writers have successively elaborated this connection into uncritically repeated statements that Cowper stayed at Freemantle House for several months in 1752 or 1755 with Sir Thomas and/or Lady Hesketh — all derived from misunderstanding of passages in the poet's later letters.

Now little read, William Cowper (1731-1800) was formerly among the most popular and oft-quoted English poets. Son of a Hertfordshire rector, he developed scholarly interests at Westminster School but from 1750 spent several frustrating years in a solicitor's office at the Inner Temple. He was called to the bar but preferred poetry to the law, writing to throw off depression. He had "an inborn inextinguishable thirst of rural scenes" but also liked visiting watering places and resorts, which in his twenties he knew as "places of idleness and luxury, music, dancing, cards, walking, riding, bathing, eating, drinking, coffee, tea, scandal, dressing, yawning, sleeping". He came to Southampton seeking recovery from a period of melancholy, arising partly from his inability to marry his fiancée, Theodora Cowper, a cousin. Her younger sister Harriet was then engaged to Thomas Hesketh (1727-78, created a baronet in 1761), whom she later married.

Resuming correspondence with this widowed lady in 1786, Cowper asked "Am I not your cousin, with whom you have wandered in the fields of Freemantle and to Bevis' Mount?" A year earlier he had written to his friend Rev. John Newton (the one-time master of a slave ship turned evangelical preacher and hymn writer, author of "Amazing Grace", who seems to have visited Southampton), "I remember Southampton well, having spent much time there; but though I was young and had no objection on the score of conscience either to dancing or cards, I never was in the assembly room in my life. I never was fond of company and especially disliked it in the country. A walk to Netley Abbey, or to Freemantle, or to Redbridge, or a book by the fireside, had always more charms for me than any other amusement that the place afforded. I was also a sailor, and being of Sir Thomas Hesketh's party, who was himself a born one, was often pressed into the service. But though I gave myself an air, and wore trowsers, I had no genuine right to that honour, disliking much to be occupied in great waters, unless in the finest weather . . . I seldom have sailed so far as from Hampton river to Portsmouth without feeling the confinement irksome and sometimes to a degree that was almost unsupportable . . . the yacht was always disagreeable to me".

From these contexts, it is clear that Cowper and his friends lodged in Southampton, then at the start of its Spa period, and that Freemantle was one of the places to which he took country walks, not the house where he stayed.

Its owner from 1822 was a man of military rather than literary distinction. General Sir George Hewett (1750-1840), who made his home for the final fifth of his long life. Son of an old Leicestershire family, he lost his parents in childhood and was entered as a cadet at Woolwich at the age of 11. A year later he became an ensign in the 70th Foot, whose colonel had been a friend of his father, and went out with this regiment to the West Indies, where he served for a decade. As a company commander in his twenties, he was sent in 1775 to North America and was involved until 1782 in the War of Independence, during which he became a major in the 43rd Foot. After some years of home service, he commanded the regiment in Ireland from 1790 and was adjutant general there in 1793-99, becoming a major general in 1796. Following various home appointments he was made a full general and served as commander-in-chief in India (1807-11) and Ireland (1813-16). His career was crowned by being created a baronet in 1818.

Freemantle House, from an engraving by G.F. Prosser, 1833. (Courtesy Southampton City Museums).

In retirement at Freemantle, the tall soldierly old man was well liked and respected. Approaching 90, he had a great desire to see the 61st regiment — of which he had been colonel for forty years — on its return to England but he died suddenly the day of its disembarkation at Southampton, March 21, 1840.

His body was placed in the catacombs beneath St. James' church, Shirley (newly built in 1836 to serve that expanding residential area) and a memorial to him was erected in the old Millbrook church of St. Nicholas, with which he had been associated, particularly in connection with its rebuilding in 1827, when he was a major contributor to the cost. The Hewett family coat of arms was later displayed on the front of the Shirley Hotel.

In 1785 Hewett married Julia Johnson, who bore him five sons and seven daughters. The former mostly followed military careers: the eldest son and heir was General Sir George Henry Hewett, who must have found himself unable to maintain the large house and estate, which he had the melancholy task of putting up for sale following the death of his mother, the Dowager Lady Hewett, in 1848, aged 86.

Another son was Lt. Col. William Henry Hewett of the Rifle Brigade, who ended his long life at his Southampton home, 17 East Park Terrace, on October 26, 1891, aged 96. Five thousand people attended his funeral, which was given full military honours because he was "the last survivor of the English officers who took part in the great battle of Waterloo in 1815" — as recorded, perhaps debatably, on his tombstone in the Old Cemetery (on the south side of the main path from the Hill Lane gate).

The sale of the Freemantle estate was entrusted to the London auctioneers Farebrother, Clark and Lye, who announced its auction for June 15, 1852, "at 12 for 1 o'clock precisely at Matcham's Royal Hotel, Southampton". The Georgian frontage of this old "posting establishment" (where Thomas Matcham was followed by several other proprietors) was an attractive feature of Above Bar until 1922, when the site was redeveloped for Woolworth's store.

Although the whole 143 acres were offered in one or 31 lots "forming most eligible sites for building purposes", the advertisements and sales particulars (preserved in Southampton Record Office) still enthused about "the distinguished and highly beautiful freehold estate" ("only about one mile and a half from the fashionable watering place of Southampton and two hours distance from London by railway" was a curious pairing of archaic and contemporary selling points) and the "excellent family residence of handsome elevation, placed in a finely timbered and richly undulated park, with beautiful lawn, pleasure grounds with umbrageous and gravelled walks, garden, hot and succession houses and grapery, lake stocked with fish, ornamental woods and plantations and rich meadow, pasture and arable lands, partly enclosed by park palings, with well arranged farming buildings".

The Hewett coat of arms adorns what is now styled "The Shirley" public house. (Photograph: Tom Holder).

The description of the "first-rate gentleman's mansion" echoed earlier accounts — "arranged with every regard to comfort, convenience and elegance . . . numerous principal and secondary bedrooms: elegant drawing room of handsome dimensions, commanding fine views, including Southampton River; a singularly beautiful dining room (the great beauty of the country) entirely formed of choice and polished marbles; library and gentleman's room . . . with a profusion of domestic offices, coach house, stabling and outbuildings". Purchasers could be "accommodated with the elegant furniture and effects as well as the farming stock, at a valuation" and were "to pay for all timber and other trees, down to the value of 1s. each inclusive".

If not sold as one lot, the estate was offered in plots — the mansion with 43 acres and thirty other lots ranging in area from one to seven acres, related to a new road proposed to be laid out, at purchasers' expense, from Shirley

Road to Foundry Lane. Included were several cottages, originally built for estate staff, and the lodges flanking the ornamental iron gates at the main entrance from Millbrook Road — now ominously annotated "either to be purchased at a valuation or will be removed". These lodges, erected for John Jarrett, had previously been much admired: they were "faced with a composition of Coade's manufacture" and decorated with bas reliefs in the same material, a form of terracotta. Millbrook Road passed through the estate, separating the main park from the smaller triangle to the south, which extended to the line of present Bourne Road, abutting on the abortive Southampton-Salisbury canal and the Southampton and Dorchester railway (opened in 1847), running along the pre-reclamation shoreline. Until renamed in 1901 to eliminate duplication after Freemantle became part of the borough, the present Cracknore Road was styled Lodge Road, being directly opposite the lodges, through which the carriage drive followed the line of Park and Waterloo Roads to the mansion, standing in the area where Mansion Road was later built across its site.

West of the house, between today's Payne's and Richmond Roads, the sale plan showed a belt of woodland and a pair of elongated lakes, fed by two streams flowing under Shirley Road and across the line of the later Firgrove Road, to meet below the present Cawte Road: the road opposite it was originally called Lake Road but in 1924 it had to give way to its Woolston namesake and was renamed Pitt Road — a change on which the Corporation insisted, despite residents' objections. Firgrove Road has kept its place on the street map; it was laid out about 1855 across what had indeed been a fir grove, on the edge of the Freemantle estate. With a frontage along Shirley Road, broken by two blocks between Waterloo and Kingston Roads owned by the Arthur Atherleys of the day (see *Streets*, chapter 3) and the corner beyond Dyer Road belonging to a Frederick Coventry, the estate boundary ran north-west along what was then Freemantle Lane (later Grove Road) and down Foundry Lane, although not including a strip along its lower section below Richmond Road, where there had been separate development.

"A view of the estate is necessary to form a correct judgement of its beauty and value" advised the auctioneers. Speculative purchasers must have had their eyes on the latter rather than the former. Foremost among them was the enterprising Sampson Payne, who took advantage of the opportunity to buy the whole Freemantle estate by private treaty ahead of the auction, for "somewhere near £20,000 including the timber" according to the *Hampshire Advertiser,* which also reported his purchase the same week of the Bugle Hall property in the old town — a very different scene but all grist to the mill for a property developer who had earlier taken up building leases on parts of the Town Marsh, drained and laid out by the Corporation from 1844.

Born at Frome in 1800, Sampson Payne established himself in 1822 at Salisbury, where he married and fathered a family of ten children. He came to Southampton in 1842 and developed his business as a china and glass merchant, with his "bazaar" at 68 High Street. By 1849 he was rich enough

Sampson Payne as Mayor, 1854-56. (Courtesy Southampton Art Gallery).

to make his home at "Clayfield", a large house off The Avenue, north of Banister Road, and to invest in land and property. He gave up shop-keeping about 1852. Payne soon became active in the public life of Southampton. He was elected a Liberal councillor for Holy Rood in 1846, moving in 1849 to All Saints, where he lost his seat in the political excitements of 1852. Winning a by-election for St. Mary's, he returned to the Council in 1854 and was unanimously chosen mayor later that year and again in 1855. He died in office, on May 22, 1856, in only his 57th year.

Even allowing for the extravagance of Victorian obituaries, Payne was clearly a popular man who served Southampton well. "His energies, his means and his genial, hearty and amiable temper were ever employed in the promotion of private happiness and the public welfare," wrote the *Hampshire Independent,* in a long account printed within heavy black rules. "His sterling qualities endeared him to all classes and parties . . . and he won golden opinions from all sorts of people. He was a sort of connecting link between conflicting parties . . . and brought persons to work harmoniously together who had too long been separated by personal misunderstandings or political differences."

The Town Council acclaimed his "unbounding munificence and untiring exertions to promote the best interests of his fellow townsmen". Payne's lavish mayoral hospitality was in the style of Richard Andrews and other successful businessmen of the time: he had also "a ready purse to aid the deserving necessitous, without parade or show". Payne was a man of strong political and religious convictions but nevertheless tolerant of other views and able to get their holders to co-operate to good purpose, moderating their divisions. Imposing in its deliberate simplicity, his funeral was the occasion for widespread public tributes. Despite heavy rain, thousands gathered at the Old Cemetery, where an open air service was conducted by Rev. Thomas Adkins, the minister of Above Bar church, of which Payne had been a deacon for many years.

Payne's early death prevented him from realising his plans for developing a large part of the Bevois Mount estate, which he bought from William Betts in 1854. Most of this was afterwards acquired by the Conservative Land Society — an ironic twist in view of Payne's prominence in local Liberal politics. Meanwhile, Payne lost little time in demolishing Freemantle House, after completing purchase of the estate by a conveyance dated September 28, 1852. Then, to quote White's 1859 Hampshire Directory, "he intersected the park by nearly twenty good roads and resold it to Land Societies and private persons, by which he realised a large profit".

Most of the area north of Richmond Road, between Firgrove Road and Foundry Lane, was acquired by the Southampton Freehold Land Society, set up in 1852 with the object of enabling members by a weekly shilling subscription to get a freehold property entitling them to the parliamentary vote — which depended upon a property qualification until 1867 and 1882 in town and country respectively. The Society's Hampshire counterpart was involved in developing the land south of Millbrook Road, which Payne initially sold to Sir John Barker Mill. Other local building societies helped in the rapid growth of Freemantle as a residential suburb, largely built up within a few years, mostly with rows of neat terraces. Census figures do not separate Freemantle and Shirley from the rest of Millbrook parish at this period but house building in Freemantle was mainly responsible for the total population increasing from 6,121 in 1851 to 10,107 in 1861, after which growth proceeded more steadily.

Ecclesiastically, Freemantle was made a separate district in 1856. The foundation stone of Christ Church was laid in 1861 and the church was consecrated in 1865; the tower and spire were added in 1875. From 1855 services were held in part of the outbuildings of Freemantle House — the laundry and brewery, which had been secured as a temporary church by Miss Charlotte Hewett, sister of the last owner of the estate. She also bought from Sampson Payne a building plot of three acres at the eastern tip of the old family property, south of Millbrook Road, and lived for a while at "Elmfield", later at houses in Bedford Place and Cumberland Place. Further adaptations converted the former bailiff's house and laundry room into a school, opened in 1857: to serve the increasing child population of the area, new buildings were erected in 1872 and 1885.

Some, if not all, of the streets laid out at Freemantle from 1853 may have been named by Sampson Payne himself. Besides those associated with the estate, they included commemoration of British victories and heroes, such as Trafalgar and Nelson, Waterloo and Wellington. The latter followed closely upon the death in 1852 of the famous "Iron Duke" (Lord Lieutenant of Hampshire from 1820). Wellington Road was renamed Wolseley Road in 1903, in compliment to Viscount Wolseley, ten years before the death of the Field Marshal whose successful campaigns in many theatres of war and army reforms made his name synonymous with order and efficiency — "All Sir Garnet" was Victorian slang for "all correct" before supplanted by the Americanism "O.K." Battles of the Crimean War were quickly celebrated at Freemantle by the naming of Alma and Varna Roads; Alma was duplicated elsewhere, hence its alteration to Almond Road in 1903.

In a different historical context, the section of Payne's Road east of Park Road was originally called Naseby Road, after the Civil War battle of 1645 when Cromwell's forces defeated the royalists. Did that Parliamentary victory retain some political significance two centuries later? Whatever the reason, this separate designation of part of a single thoroughfare proved confusing, so in 1904 Payne's Road was applied to its whole length.

Overleaf: The sale plan of the Freemantle estate.

From Romsey & Shirley
Tithing of Hill and Sidford
Tithing of Millbrook
F. COVENTRY, ESQ.
Stream
SOLD TO Mr A. PETTY
SOLD TO FREEHOLD LAND SOCIETY
WELLINGTON ROAD
ALBANY ROAD
NELSON ROAD
RICHMOND ROAD
FOUNDRY LANE
From Shirley
Graperey
Conservatory
Paths
Ornamental
From Salisbury, Lyndhurst, & the New Forest
MILBROOK
SOLD TO SIR
Public Footpath
DORCHESTER
QUAY
THE SOUTHA

GRACE
ROAD
19
20
21
22
23
24
WATERLOO ROAD
To Southampton
To Southampton
SOLD TO 25 H. PAGE, ESQ.
Drive
Entrance Gates
SOLD TO MISS HEWETT
BARBER MILL, BART.
Canal
Salisbury
RAILWAY
Public Footpath
TON WATER

Victorian respect for royalty was expressed in the naming of Prince's Road and Queen's Road; the latter was expanded into Queenstown Road in 1903 to distinguish it from another in Shirley. Richmond Road may have harked back to the earl who became Henry VII; Albany was both a ducal title and the ancient poetic name for north Britain.

South of Millbrook Road, earlier history was exemplified by Saxon and Norman Roads — flanking the railway — while above them other roads were named Elgin and Waverley. The latter took the title of Sir Walter Scott's novel, first published in 1814 and immensely popular for many years. Elgin Road memorialised the seventh Earl of Elgin (1766-1841), whose diplomatic career was highlighted by bringing to England the friezes from the Parthenon at Athens and other "Elgin Marbles". These were acquired for the British Museum in 1816 after a Commons committee endorsed the propriety of their removal — the subject of controversy then, as now, when Greece is seeking their return: in Elgin's day, the Greeks were ruled by the Turks, with whom he arranged matters. Was the naming of Elgin Road prompted by thoughts of the Italian marbles which John Jarrett had imported to adorn Freemantle House?

Sir George's Road was an unusual style of street name, chosen to honour the baronet general Hewett but Hewitt's Road curiously perpetuated an error in spelling his surname, which seems to have been common in local newspapers and directories even during his lifetime.

The larger of the two ornamental lakes that enhanced the estate landscape in Hewett's day survived a century longer than the "big house". In Victorian times the occupiers of houses in Richmond and Payne's Roads, with gardens backing on to it, enjoyed private access to walks around it, paying ten shillings a year for the maintenance of this amenity. Five and a half acres were reserved as public open space in 1938 and in 1956-58 the lake was filled in to make a recreation ground, offically opened on October 8, 1958.

As a feature of Georgian park layout, the lakes were developed out of an older mill pond. The OS map of 1867 still showed Mill House to the north-east of the lake and the nearby "Old Ice House" — a survivor from pre-refrigeration times when winter ice was collected and stored in insulated underground chambers, keeping it available for the gentry's kitchens and tables throughout the year.

Ice houses merit a short digression. Most large "country" houses had their own in the 18th and 19th centuries. The one at Mottisfont Abbey, restored by the National Trust, is the best local example. Forty other Hampshire survivals, in varying states of preservation, were listed by Monica Ellis in her history of "Ice and Ice Houses" published in 1982 by Southampton University Industrial Archaeology Group.

The first Freemantle School, about 1860. (Courtesy Godfrey Cawte).

Traces have long since vanished of those formerly serving Freemantle, Bevois Mount and old Portswood House, while one at Sholing was dug out and demolished in 1952-53, its site becoming the front gardens of new houses at the bottom of Spring Road — which older residents still called Ice House Hill. Originally part of William Chamberlayne's Weston Grove estate but detached from it when the eastern section was sold in 1854 to Robert Wright for "Mayfield", this was set into the bank opposite Miller's Pond, which was once larger, providing enough ice for the Royal Mail company to use it for supplying its ships from the 1860s until late Victorian times, when it was superseded by bulk importations from North America and Norway. There were several commercial ice pits off the High Street, French Street and Back of the Walls.

An earlier town ice house was built in the late 18th century by Grantham Knight at the foot of the old castle hill and sold in 1798 to Robert Miller, a pastry cook who presumably specialised in ice confections. In 1805 "Miller's Ice House" was bought for £100 by the Marquis of Lansdowne, as an adjunct of the mock castle he built on the hill that bears his name (see *Streets*, pages 23-28). Like contemporary country mansions, his "Gothick Folly" would thus have had its own year-round ice supply for preserving food, chilling wine and making novel cold desserts. This ice house probably disappeared when the short-lived "castle" was demolished in 1818.

The Ice House Inn in Warren Avenue (also once popularly known as Ice House Hill) has a history barely hinted at by its igloo signboard. It was built in 1912 over a large disused ice pit, which had been constructed about 1850 for Thomas Cozens, owner of the Clarence Hotel and an adjoining fish shop in the High Street. Brick-walled and 25 ft. deep, surmounted by a thick covering of earth, it was sited immediately north of the west end of Shirley Ponds — which used to stretch almost from Warren Avenue to Romsey Road: their area shrank through silting and was greatly reduced by the Corporation filling in the western stretch of water for a recreation area in 1963.

Old Mill Way recalls the mill worked for centuries by the head of water built up from the meeting of Hollybrook and Tanners Brook. A change of use came by 1806, when the first OS map marked it as Shirley Iron Foundry: in 1809 John Bullar described it as "a manufactory of iron spades and shovels (where) the laborious process of flattening the metal is expedited by means of a large hammer worked by a water wheel". The mill was not shown as a foundry on the Shirley enclosure map of 1830, so its operation may have been intermittent. In 1843 the Millbrook tithe map and schedule recorded Joseph Till occupying "Shirley Mill Iron Works", with 14½ acres of meadows, feeding streams and ponds. Ten years later, Messrs. Hughes and Tillott were listed there but soon afterwards the buildings were sold to a brewer, William Brown. The brewery continued under various ownerships and was taken over in 1899 by the Winchester Brewery. In 1900 the premises were acquired by the Royal

Mail company and used for their ships' laundry until this transferred to the Docks about 1920. They were demolished in 1959 and the site is now used for car sales.

The more extensive area of Shirley Ponds a century ago yielded plenty of ice, to be cut out and packed down in the ice pit, for later delivery to hotels, better-off householders, dealers in perishable foods and steamship companies. In hard winters there was still enough to allow impromptu fairs to be held on the thick pond ice, where bonfires were sometimes lit! The Shirley Warren pit also received ice shipped from abroad and brought from the Docks by horse-drawn vans for storing until required by customers. To cater for the thirsty carters and ice house workers, a house nearby became a beer house about 1880. The original Ice House Inn, to the north of its 1912 successor, reverted to domestic use but traces of its painted name could still be seen on its brick frontage until this was rendered over a few years ago. The former ice pit, partly filled in, now serves as a cellar for storing beer instead of ice.

Returning to Freemantle, the 1867 OS map also showed the disused mill race or leet cut straight from the western tip of the lake towards the foundry which gave the name to Foundry Lane and the remains of the old wharf that served it — at the bottom of the lane, across Millbrook Road near the railway station. Both wharf and foundry have long since disappeared through land reclamation and redevelopment. The foundry occupied the area between modern Lakelands Drive, Somerset Terrace and 5-47 Foundry Lane. Successor to an earlier corn mill, it probably came into being during the Napoleonic Wars and was first noted in 1809 by John Bullar, who wrote that "immediately below Freemantle House, on the right, an iron foundry makes its appearance". Other guide books of the following decade mentioned "Mill Place foundry and beyound it a road leading to Shirley Common and Romsey Road". Foundry Lane was listed (under Millbrook) in the Southampton directory of 1834, which recorded the occupiers of three country houses, the foundry and "Foundry Cottage".

The first operators of the foundry remain uncertain but St. Nicholas church rate book (preserved in the City Record Office) shows that Charles and Henry Tickell took it over in 1818, apparently from a man named Plunkett. The Tickells' tenure was tragically short but notable for the production of the handsome cast iron "Gas Column" (see *Streets*, page 68) that now stands on the traffic island at the busy junction of Queensway with Hanover Buildings and Houndwell Place. Passers-by can admire the Southampton arms adorning two sides of the base and read the inscription on the others — "erected by subscription as a tribute of respect and gratitude to William Chamberlayne Esq., for his munificent gift of the iron columns supporting the public lights of the town" — but they may easily overlook the lettering identifying the makers, "Tickells, founder, Southampton". (See next page.)

A directory dated 1823 still listed "Tickell and Co., iron founders,

Millbrook" but by then the two principals were both dead. Their name first appeared in the parish register in November 1818, recording the baptism of the infant son of Charles and Elizabeth Tickell — and his burial only five days later. Other tragedies struck the Tickells, for in September 1820 the *Hampshire Chronicle* reported the death of Henry Tickell, aged 29, "at his house at the iron foundry . . . in consequence of being thrown from his gig near his house and being thereby most dreadfully mutilated". Twelve months later, Charles Tickell (presumably his brother) was also dead, at only 33, no cause being this time noted. By September 1821, the foundry must already have been engaged in producing the Gas Column. Was this very accomplished and complicated job finished by the Tickells' workmen, while the widowed Mrs. Tickell (or two of them) carried on the firm for a while? Mrs. Tickell was still paying church rates on the foundry in 1824, before Alexander Fletcher and John Young took over. Perhaps they operated it for her before becoming its owners?

The Gas Column stood on the Town Quay from 1829 to 1865 as shown in Philip Brannon's engraving of 1850.

In May, 1822 the "subscription column" was reported "nearly complete". The first stone of "the basis for supporting it" was laid by the mayor, George Atherley, on July 24 and the column was set up a few days later, at the junction of New Road and Above Bar, then regarded as "the entrance to the town".

Connecting the gas took some time, until it was lighted for the first time on January 4, 1823. Initially there were four lamps, "to the four points of the compass, conspicuous at a great distance". In 1825, "to make it a more distinguished object", they were replaced by a large single lamp — "and exceedingly brilliant was the effect".

Fletcher and Young operated the Mill Place Foundry for seven years, their business extending from supplying guttering for the rebuilt church of St. Nicholas (Fletcher, who lived with his family at Foundry Cottage, was involved in church affairs, serving in 1827 on the vestry committee allocating pews according to size of subscription to the rebuilding fund) to making steam engines for early paddle steamers. In 1831 the foundry was bought by the partnership of Ogle and Summers, who moved from Whitechapel where they had patented and constructed "steam engines and other boilers or generators applicable to propelling vessels, locomotive carriages and to other purposes". Their steam-propelled road carriages ran around London streets and made journeys to Brentford, Basingstoke and Southampton. The partners gave evidence to a House of Commons committee in 1831, claiming speeds of 30 m.p.h. for their 3-ton coke-fired carriage, which could carry twenty passengers.

Captain Nathaniel Ogle R.N. (presumably retired) came of an extensive family centred in Northumberland and Hampshire, with numerous members prominent in navy, army and church. He may have been the son of the man of the same name recorded in directories of 1803-11 living in Orchard Place — who was probably the one buried at St. Mary Extra, Pear Tree Green, in 1813, aged 47. The Millbrook church rate book shows Nathaniel Ogle living in the parish in 1828 but not in 1829-31, when he was evidently involved with Summers at their Whitechapel foundry. Ogle's Millbrook connection was exemplified by his placing in St. Nicholas church a tablet to the memory of his mother — although her burial there is not recorded; this was executed by Edward Hodges Bailey R.A., a sculptor of some repute in his day.

William Alltoft Summers was a talented engineer: Captain Ogle probably joined him primarily as a provider of capital but he was also an intrepid driver of the firm's steam carriages. Established in Foundry Lane, where Summers made Foundry Cottage his home, the partners lost little time in putting a new machine on the road to Winchester in the first days of 1832. It had to stop two miles short because of too much head of steam but later it drew a 2-ton boiler and thirty people to Eling and did a round trip to Romsey — at a sedate 12 m.p.h., with a dozen brave ladies among the passengers.

In September 1832 a second improved steam carriage took 22 people to Oxford and Birmingham. "The desideratum of a moving power, by which carriages can be propelled on the common roads of the country with speed and safety and without smoke" attracted admiring crowds and enthusiastic accounts. It was reported that "during its first progress there was considerable difficulty in regulating the speed downhill, the machine having in one instance hurried down a declivity at a most enormous rate, probably 50 miles an hour. Captain Ogle, by his nerve and management steered it, notwithstanding, with perfect ease". This fault was amended and on other stretches of road more modest speeds of 10-14 m.p.h. were maintained.

Summers must, however, have recognised that the future lay with railways, not with "steam locomotion on common roads". Ogle was last recorded at Millbrook in the 1834 directory. After his departure (or death?) the firm was styled "W.A. Summers and Co., engineers and iron founders, Millbrook Foundry" until the principal found a new partner in Charles Day (1776-1849), to whom he was introduced by the banker Martin Maddison (see *Streets*, pages 30 and 54). Day's eldest son, Charles Arthur Day (1816-92), joined Summers as a working partner. Other men were also involved in the company — John Groves of Millbrook from 1836 and William Baldock a decade later. Their

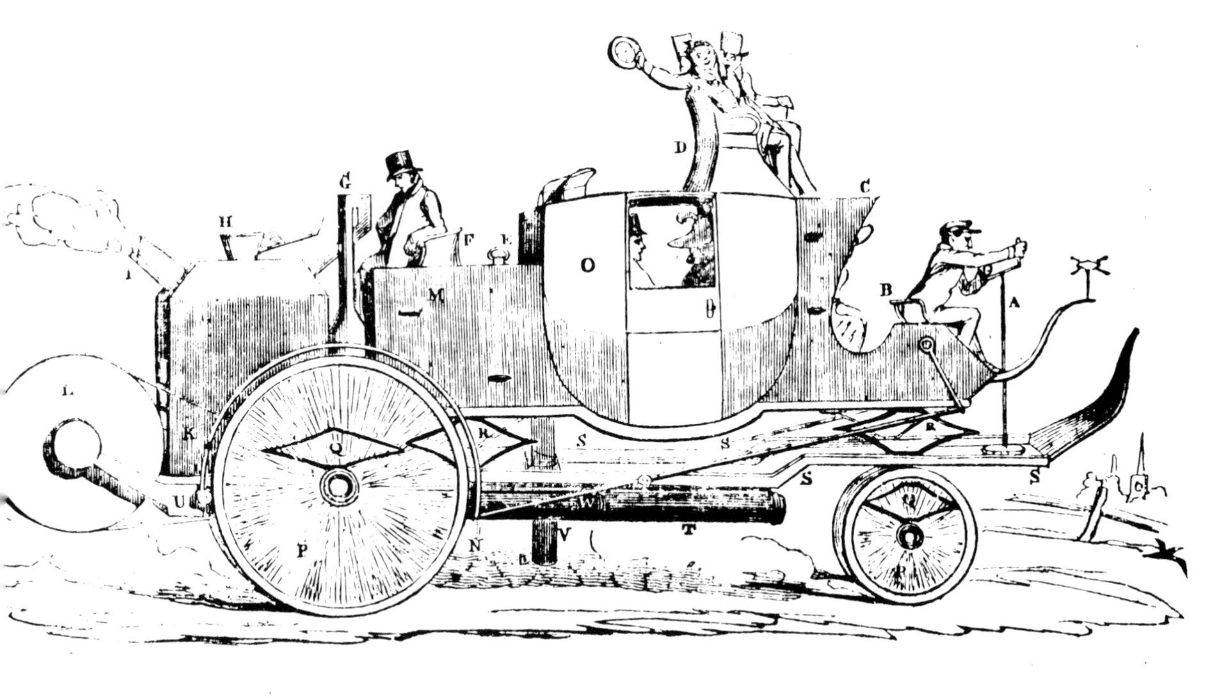

"A correct representation of Messrs. Ogle and Summers's Steam Carriage" – an illustration from the Dublin Literary Journal of 1832.

names featured briefly in the firm's title, which, after several changes (e.g. Summers and Day in the 1850s and C.A. Day and Co. in the 1860s) became fixed as Day, Summers and Co. from 1871.

Turning from road to rail, in 1837-39 Summers, Groves and Day ("steam engine manufacturers") built at least four railway locomotives. The "Jefferson" was exported to Virginia; another was sold to the LSWR. In June 1839 a "beautiful engine of 10 h.p." made a trial run on the new Southampton-Winchester line and in August a more powerful 6-wheel locomotive called "Southampton" was placed in service on it.

Meanwhile, the firm was increasingly engaged in making marine engines and boilers, from which Summers went on to build his first iron steamship, the 20-ton *Forester*, launched from Mill Place Quay in 1836. Vessels built at the Millbrook Foundry had to be dragged across the Millbrook Road for launching. In March 1839 local newpapers reported road traffic held up for several days while another larger iron steamship (about 120 tons) was moved to its launching place. To avoid these disadvantages, the firm secured a new site on the Itchen, just below Northam Bridge, and there developed its Northam Iron Works. From there, its first launch was the *Pride of the Waters*, a paddle steamer for the Isle of Wight service, on October 14, 1840. For a while the company continued engineering work at Millbrook but in 1854 it closed its foundry there and concentrated on ship building and marine engine making at Northam. It produced a steady sequence of iron steamers, both screw and paddle types, of increasing size, for the P. and O., Union, Royal Mail and Hamburg America lines. The largest was the *Hindostan*, 3,113 tons, in 1869.

The founder's changes of address reflected his business success. By 1850 he occupied the first house in new and fashionable Denzil Avenue; a few years later he moved to Ridgemount House, Bassett — still described in directories as "civil engineer" but now rating "esquire" after his name. He died in 1862, having retired to Hull, his home town. In 1871 C.A. Day was succeeded by his son Arthur James Day (1847-1923) and Thomas Summers (1826-89) became co-principal with him.

Coming to Southampton about 1842 to work for William Summers, his cousin and later brother-in-law, Thomas Summers developed his talents as mechanical engineer, naval architect and inventor. In 1862 he patented with C.A. Day a new type of traversing sheerlegs for lifting weights of up to 200 tons. Over a hundred sets were subsequently made at the Northam Iron Works and supplied to docks and shipbuilding yards all over the world, along with others mounted on self-propelled floating pontoons. Other Summers and Day patents of 1879-84 covered steam-driven wire rope hauling-up slipway machinery, to handle ships of up to 3,500 tons; scores of these slipway sets were exported from Northam to many countries.

From the 1870s, shipbuilding on a larger scale centred in northern yards but the Northam Iron Works built many long-lasting smaller steamers and tugs, while also extending its engineering and ship repair works. In 1888 Day, Summers and Co. built a submarine torpedo boat to the specification of an American consortium. The *Incognita* proved an ill-fated venture, sinking at her mooring soon after being handed over in 1889 — through no fault of her builders, as a law suit later established. In 1892-96 the firm built two steam floating bridges for the Itchen chain ferry: a third was the last construction job undertaken by Day, Summers and Co. in 1928. Meanwhile, another speciality came to the fore among the firm's activities in the decades either side of 1900, when numerous luxury steam yachts were built and fitted out at Northam.

When Thomas Summers died at his Winn Road home in 1889, he was survived by four sons. At least two of them, William and Thomas, were involved

Opposite: G. Buxey's town map, about 1883, shows Freemantle largely built up while much of Shirley is yet undeveloped.

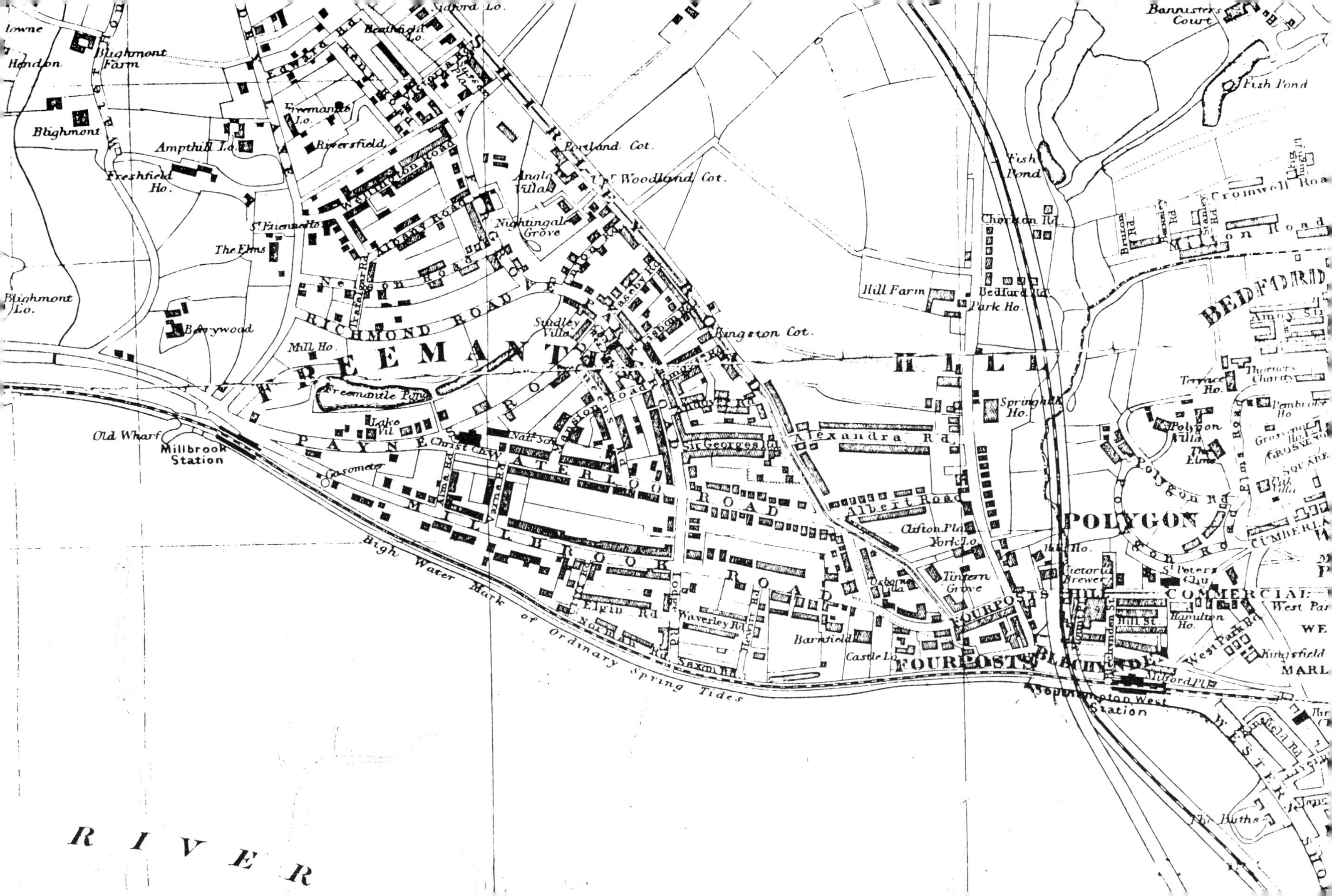
FREEMANTLE
HILL
POLYGON
BEDFORD
FOURPOSTS
FOURPOSTS HILL
COMMERCIAL
RICHMOND ROAD
PAYNE
WATERLOO ROAD
MILLBROOK ROAD
SHIRLEY ROAD
Alexandra Rd.
Albert Road
Sir Georges
Waverley Rd
Elgin Rd
Norman Rd
Lodge Rd
Nelson Road
Wellington Road
Edward Rd
Cromwell Road
Milton Road
Bruton Rd
Polygon Rd
Hill St.
West Park Rd
Milford Pl.
High Water Mark of Ordinary Spring Tides
RIVER
Old Wharf
Millbrook Station
Southampton West Station
Blighmont
Blighmont Farm
Blighmont Lo.
Hendon
Ampthill Lo.
Freshfield Ho.
The Elms
Baywood
Mill Ho.
Fremantle Pond
Lake Vil.
Christ Chy.
Gasometer
Riversfield
Nightingale Grove
Portland Cot.
Woodland Cot.
Kingston Cot.
Sidford Lo.
Hill Farm
Bedford Rd.
Park Ho.
Charlton Rd.
Fish Pond
Bannisters Court
Springhill Ho.
Terrace Ho.
Polygon Villa
Clifton Pl.
York Lo.
Tintern Grove
Osborne Villa
Barnfield
Castle Lo.
Hamilton Ho.
Kingsfield
St. Peters Chy.
The Baths

with Arthur Payne in building racing yachts from the 1890s at other yards on the Itchen. A.J. Day retired in 1914 but soon returned to direct the firm during World War I, when his eldest son, Colonel Campbell Day, was away on active service. He was one of ten children: his younger brother Captain Owen Day was killed at Gallipoli. A.J. Day is also remembered as a cricketer, donor of the club competition trophy that bears his name. As a young man, he played for county sides and later formed his own team, called the Northlands Rovers (from the name of his home, Northlands House, built in 1881 and now an old people's home): out of this team grew the Hampshire Hogs C.C., which celebrated its centenary in 1987.

Day, Summers and Co. closed down in 1929, when their Northam yard was taken over by Thornycrofts, but a reminder of the firm's significant contribution to shipbuilding and engineering developments in Southampton and of the founder of its forerunner at Freemantle over a century and a half ago survives in the naming of Summers Street. Running between Northam Road and Radcliffe Road, this was originally Albert Street, one of several named in compliment to the Prince Consort. To reduce this duplication, the Borough Council altered it to Summers Street in 1901.

SHIRLEY MILLS BREWERY

Westwood House and Mr. Winn

William Winn's name has been perpetuated on the suburban street scene for over a century, commemorating the man responsible for laying out Winn and Westwood Roads across the park of Westwood House, the estate which he bought and divided up into house building plots from 1880.

Westwood House was probably created out of an older farm house. South Stoneham parish rate books show Westwood and other property owned in the 1780s by Richard Elcock, presumably the man of that name buried at the parish church in 1803. The "translation" of farm into country house probably took place about 1805, for Westwood House is shown on the Ordnance Survey maps of 1808-10 although not on John Doswell's 1802 map of Southampton and district, which shows most of the country houses around the then outskirts of the town. Westwood House may have been built for a certain Joseph Tomkins, despite the fact that the "Southampton Register" of 1811 listed him at nearby Portswood House: this may have been a compiler's error or perhaps he then held both properties. For most of the decade from 1816 Westwood House was the home of Admiral Robert Waller Otway (1770-1846), who merits his place in the Dictionary of National Biography.

Son of an Irish Ascendancy family, he entered the Royal Navy at 14 and saw service in many ships and waters, with particular distinction in actions off the West Indies in 1795-1800, when he had "a singularly adventurous and successful career". In six years he is credited with capturing or destroying some two hundred enemy privateers and merchant ships, while successively commanding the 32-36 gun frigates *Mermaid, Ceres* and *Trent.* The latter in 1799-1800, according to one naval historian, "is supposed to have made as many captures as ever fell to the lot of one vessel in the same space of time". After various other commands in the Baltic and Mediterranean, he was promoted Rear Admiral in 1814.

His residence at Westwood House was interrupted by his appointment as Commander-in-Chief at Leith in 1818-21, during which time the house was leased to Thomas Penruddock Mitchell. South Stoneham parish register records the christening of three children of "Robert Waller and Clementina Otway, Portswood, Rear Admiral" — their son, George, in 1816, a daughter, Caroline Letitia, in 1817 and another son, Edward, in 1824. In 1826, Otway was knighted and appointed C. in C. on the South American station.

He thereupon gave up his Southampton estate, which was taken by George Alexander Fullerton. He enlarged it by securing more land on the Portswood side and removing the farm buildings to the south-east corner — beside the cut between Westwood Road and Gordon Avenue. As extended, Westwood House park comprised some 43 acres, its boundaries running on the north along the backs of the gardens of the later Winn Road (abutting the grounds of Highfield House) and on the south between the gardens of the future Westwood Road and Gordon Avenue (backing on to the Bevois Mount estate, as Henry Hulton had enlarged it about 1810); eastward, the Westwood grounds reached the line of Brookvale Road. Westwood House itself stood approximately on the sites of Nos. 15, 17, 19 Winn Road.

Fullerton, who also owned properties in Gloucestershire and County Antrim, may have leased Westwood House around 1839 but he and his family, attended by thirteen resident servants, were recorded there on census night in the spring of 1841. Soon afterwards, the estate was put up for sale — through the enterprising agency of Charles Brooks, of 8 Above Bar Street, whose advertisements proclaimed him not only "the oldest-established auctioneer, house agent, appraiser and yacht agent, agent to the Phoenix Fire and Eagle Life Offices" but also wine, ale and porter merchant; to these businesses was added "the Funeral Furnishing Department conducted with Respectful Attention and Strict Economy".

A copy of the Westwood House estate particulars issued by Mr. Brooks is preserved in the Southampton Record Office. He waxed eloquent in describing "this splendid modern villa and freehold estate of 43 acres of rich park-like land on the high London road, 1½ mile from Southampton". He proclaimed that "this extremely elegant villa is the residence and property of a gentleman who has lately expended considerable sums to render it in every way perfect and suitable for the reception of a family of the first distinction and which in point of situation, convenience, desirability and comfort can but seldom be met with and rarely equalled. This delightful residence is encompassed by a lawn on which is placed a conservatory and the shrubberies, which are in great profusion, are intersected by beautiful walks displaying superior taste in the arrangements. It is finely seated in a park richly studded with timber trees and for beauty of scenery not to be surpassed by any in this or the adjoining counties, as the grounds are laid out in a manner that must gratify every beholder and the most fastidious will give to the artist the merit so justly due to him".

Moreover, "what renders this admired estate so valuable is its being the only freehold of the kind so near the beautiful and enchanting town and river of Southampton and in the neighbourhood of Highfield and Portswood, surrounded by beautiful and park-like grounds and adorned by many elegant seats and villas, the residences and properties of the first class of society, and bounded by two excellent roads".

In fact, the Westwood grounds did not quite extend to The Avenue or Portswood Road ("Southton to Winton" on the Brooks sale plan) and the house was approached from each side by carriage drives off the main roads — the first at approximately the line of Winn Road, swinging north and east;

The former Westwood farm cottage, beside the cut between Gordon Avenue and Westwood Road.

and the second along the line of the eastern end of Gordon Avenue and up into what became Westwood Road, then around the eastern edge of the estate to the "big house". Mr. Brooks drew attention to this being "seated on an elevated and commanding spot" and noted that "at its approach (from The Avenue) is a tasty entrance lodge and beautiful carriage drive through the shrubberies".

The agent's engravings and plan were complemented by his copperplate folio description of the house, noting its "elegant entrance hall, with handsome stone staircase; elegant drawing room with three windows opening under a veranda to the lawn; dining room, morning room, parlour and study and a conveniently placed water closet".

Over half the ground floor was taken up by the servants' quarters, including "an excellent kitchen fitted with every convenience". On the first floor, approached by two staircases, were "ten excellent bedrooms, with two large dressing rooms and water closet. A postscript rather quaintly underlined that "the best as well as the servants' bedrooms and offices have each a fireplace". Two large bedrooms for servants "to contain 8 beds" were in a separate building, above the "large lofty laundry, brew and wash-house". In addition, "the outdoor premises and offices, which are very superior, consist of a large stable yard enclosed by a high brick wall, a capital coach house for 3 carriages, with a loft over; a large and lofty 7 stalled stable, excellent harness room and man servants' bedroom spacious enough for 4 beds".

In July, 1841 the Westwood estate was bought by William Byam (later Sir William). He lived there intermittently, sometimes letting the house on short tenancies. The Southampton directories of 1843-45 showed it as the residence of John Hopton Forbes, before he left to establish himself at Merry Oak. William Byam was listed as owner and occupier of Westwood under the South Stoneham tithe award of 1845. Two years later, its previous owner, G.A. Fullerton, left £360 in 3% stock to that church, in trust for the dividends to be distributed to poor parishioners, after meeting the upkeep of his family tomb.

The 1851 census recorded John Vignoles at Westwood, with his wife Louisa and seven living-in servants. Then 58, he was a Royal Navy lieutenant, retired on half pay — of Irish origin but with local connections dating back at least to 1820, when he was elected an honorary burgess of Southampton. He left Westwood about 1855 to take a lease of Archers Lodge, the house in The Avenue which the sisters of La Sainte Union bought in 1880 to open their Convent High School. Westwood House stood empty at the time of the 1861 census. The 1865 directory recorded George Atherley there but the tenancy of this Southampton banker (see *Streets*, page 34) was evidently brief, as his name did not re-appear in the 1867 list.

Directories of 1869-71 again recorded Sir William Byam at Westwood House;

Westwood House, 1872. (Courtesy Southampton Record Office).

in fact, he died in July, 1869 and his widow did not long survive him. By order of Sir William's executors, the estate was put up for auction by Mr. W. Furber (of Hyde Park and Southampton) at the Royal Hotel, Above Bar on July 4, 1872.

The sale particulars of "this charming freehold estate" — still described as "within 1½ miles of Southampton" — lauded (less fulsomely than by Mr. Brooks in 1841) the attractions of the "modern freehold residence, very substantially built and of good elevation, standing upon high ground, in an extremely healthy situation, being built upon a gravel sub-soil, commanding pleasant views of the surrounding country, placed in the midst of tastefully laid out shrubberies and flower gardens and surrounded by park-like meadows of about 44½ acres" with "very superior out-door premises and offices, walled and well-stocked kitchen garden and farm buildings comprising a bailiff's cottage, with accommodation for 10 cows and horses, cart sheds etc.".

WESTWOOD, SOUTHAMPTON.

The Particulars and Conditions of Sale

OF A CHARMING

FREEHOLD ESTATE,

KNOWN AS

"WESTWOOD,"

Within 1½ Miles of Southampton, the

MODERN FREEHOLD RESIDENCE,

Which is very substantially built, and of good elevation. It is placed in the midst of TASTEFULLY-LAID-OUT

SHRUBBERIES AND FLOWER GARDENS,

And surrounded by

PARK-LIKE MEADOWS OF ABOUT 44½ ACRES.

THE HOUSE IS APPROACHED BY A

Lodge Entrance, through a beautiful belt of Choice Trees and Shrubs.

THE

OUT-DOOR PREMISES AND OFFICES,

Which are very superior, consist of a Large STABLE YARD, enclosed by a Brick Wall,

A capital COACH HOUSE for 4 Carriages, with a Loft over,

A LARGE AND LOFTY 7-STALL STABLE,

A LARGE LAUNDRY, BREW AND WASH-HOUSES,

WALLED & WELL-STOCKED KITCHEN GARDEN.

To be SOLD by AUCTION, by

MR. W. FURBER

(By order of the Executors of the late Sir WILLIAM BYAM),

On THURSDAY, JULY 4th, 1872,

AT THE

ROYAL HOTEL, ABOVE BAR, SOUTHAMPTON,

AT THREE o'CLOCK.

Further particulars to be obtained of Messrs. SHARP, HARRISON & POCOCK, Solicitors, Southampton; Mr. J. FURBER, Auctioneer, 1, Southwick Street, Hyde Park, London; or of the Auctioneer, 22, Above Bar, Southampton, of whom Tickets may be had to view.

PAUL & SON, Printers, High Street, Southampton.

Mr. Furber noted that "the residence has always been occupied by families of distinction and would give any gentleman owning it a large amount of local influence. Three packs of hounds meet within easy distance, with excellent yachting and fishing near, railway accommodation to all parts of England, and steam ditto to all parts of the world, and within 2½ hours of London, altogether forming one of the most complete residences in the neighbourhood".

Perhaps more to the point, he wrote that "it also offers many attractions to the speculator, being placed in one of the most charming spots in this beautiful neighbourhood. It is certain in a few years to become very valuable for building purposes".

Perhaps because Victorian prosperity was temporarily in recession, bidding at the auction was slow and the property had to be bought in at £14,000. A year later it was purchased privately by the man designated in leases and conveyances of the 1880s as "William Winn Esq. of Haddo House, Bow, Middlesex" — of whom more later. Westwood House was then taken on a short lease by Sir Charles Harvey; he was listed only in the 1874 directory, along with "Charles Herbert, gardener, Westwood Park Lodge". The last tenant of the mansion was Mrs. Margaret Sullivan. She died in January, 1876, aged 78, and afterwards the old house seems to have remained empty.

Within a few years, Winn was ready to proceed with his development plans, involving demolition of Westwood House. On February 14, 1879, the Borough Council's Common committee was informed that Winn had instructed Messrs. Pearce, Paris and Smith, in conjunction with James Lemon, to lay out the Westwood Park estate. Mr. Paris and Mr. Lemon attended to seek Corporation consent to roads involving rights of way across the strip of Common land down the east side of The Avenue. The committee agreed, requiring Mr. Winn to pay £200 for these rights and making the condition that each new house should have a minimum value of £600. A month later, councillors were told that he resisted the charge and said that if the Corporation insisted he would be compelled to alter his plans and let off the land in smaller allotments, "permitting the erection of second and third rate houses".

The committee was persuaded to charge only £100 for widening the right of way for Winn Road and granting a new access to form Westwood Road.

Winn's agent in Southampton was Alexander Paris, who began selling building plots on long leases, with covenants ensuring that they were used only for erection of private dwelling houses "to be built in good substantial and workmanlike manner with all the best materials of all sorts". Quality control was further effected by specifying they should be of a minimum value, up to £1,000 for detached villas in Winn Road on plots measuring 60 by 180 feet; plots were narrower in Westwood Road, where some semi-detached pairs were erected.

Paris himself had one of the first houses built in Winn Road — number 5, called "Twynham", where he lived till 1899. By 1887 about a score of houses had been built in Westwood Road and a dozen in Winn Road. Initially these were concentrated along the north side of the latter and the south side of the former, because in 1883 Winn had granted a 14-year lease of a ten acre block between these roads to the Royal Southampton Horticultural Society, for use as pleasure and show grounds. The Society, established in 1862 and given the title "Royal" by the Queen's command in 1878, was then flourishing with some 1,200 members. It paid a rent of £50 for the first year from March 1, 1883 and £75 p.a. thereafter.

The Society held its first show there in June, 1883, having by then laid out a cinder track and two tennis courts. Facilities were gradually increased to 11 courts and "a splendid running track", with a grandstand on its north side and a bandstand to the west of it (as shown on the OS map of 1897). The Westwood Park grounds were made available to neighbouring residents for £5 or up to a guinea a year for use of the tennis courts. They were also used for various special events, notably on June 22, 1887 for Queen Victoria Jubilee celebrations, when 10,000 people were reported to have attended the displays and sports, including a race for "veterans" born before 1837. The next afternoon, thousands of children were entertained at Westwood Park. Other special occasions there included the "fete on a grand scale, in grounds brilliantly illuminated" in connection with the Royal Counties Agricultural Show held at Southampton in June, 1893.

Two years later, the Society decided not to seek renewal of its lease, expiring in 1897. Its report noted "the closing of Westwood Park will undoubtedly be a great public loss but it has not proved the financial success anticipated". In any case, the lease might not have been renewed, for by 1897 (Paris having bought the remainder of the estate from Winn in 1894), Winn and Westwood Roads were almost fully built up along their outer sides, with some houses at The Avenue end already filling the plots backing each other between the two roads. By 1907 they were almost completely built up, with about sixty houses in Westwood Road and forty in Winn Road. After the departure of the Horticultural Society, the tennis courts were used by members of the Westwood Park LTC, until it closed soon after World War I.

Winn and Westwood Roads were favoured by successful business and professional men, like Walter Mayes, Edward Bance and Sir Russell Bencraft. The years between the wars saw gradual changes, with large houses divided into flats or used for what planners called "institutional" purposes, such as Sister Wright's private nursing home. This process was hastened during World War II, when many houses were taken over for military occupation or as offices by firms bombed out of the city centre. More recently, the sites of about half the original late Victorian villas have been redeveloped with blocks of flats or old people's homes — mostly styled "Court" and bearing names like Ranelagh, Pembroke and Buckingham, even Elfin.

Dr. David Lockhart and his wife.

More distinctive and significant is the name of David Lockhart Court, at the Brookvale Road end of Westwood Road, a block of flats for the elderly completed in 1984, with the involvement of Portswood Evangelical Church. Its elders named it to perpetuate the memory of the respected doctor who lived nearby in Brookvale Road and for many years devoted himself to its ministry and activities. Dr. Lockhart came to Southampton in 1933 to take a post at the Royal South Hants Hospital. In 1944, he was instrumental in the church acquiring 76 Westwood Road (bought at auction for £1,250) as a centre for Christian service to the troops then thronging the area, which was an assembly point for men and vehicles gathering to embark for Normandy. The church house actually opened its doors on D-Day.

It afterwards developed as a youth centre, extended by purchase of the adjoining house, 78 Westwood Road, in 1967. Ten years later, under an imaginative redevelopment scheme, the church sold the properties to the Baptist Men's Movement Housing Association, thus financing the provision of a manse and extensions to its buildings in Portswood Road to unify its young people's activities there and at the same time enabling the Association to build flats for the elderly in Westwood Road, on similar lines to its first scheme in Southampton — Kingsland Court, on the site of the former Kingsland Baptist Church. Dr. Lockhart (who retired in 1970 and died in 1980) always shunned the limelight for himself. But with the agreement of his widow, the Portswood Church Fellowship unanimously decided to recognise his life of service by giving his name to the new building, which Mrs. Lockhart formally opened in March, 1985.

The houses, 76, 78, 80 Westwood Road (supplemented by a corrugated iron assembly hall known familiarly as the "tin tabernacle") had earlier accommodated New College, a private school for girls established about 1892 by Miss Knight and taken over around 1900 by Miss Agnes Allnutt, a forceful lady who had studied Classics to Honours level at Oxford, where women were then still denied the award of degrees. Her name afforded obvious possibilities for facetious schoolgirl variations but "The Nutt" was both feared and respected by her "young ladies" — daughters of gentlemen, not tradesmen, for she "drew the line at shutters". Miss Allnutt took into partnership Miss Trist and they ran a successful school for both day pupils and boarders until retiring about 1920. Miss Mary Dawson continued New College for another five years, until shrinking numbers, reflecting increased local authority provision of secondary education for girls, obliged her to close it in 1925.

"Old Girls" of New College included an entrant of 1904, later Mrs. McHaffie, the daughter of Mrs. Foster Welch. When her mother made civic history by becoming Southampton's first woman mayor in 1927, she served as mayoress. Her contemporary, Elsie Sandell, made herself synonymous with the history of Southampton.

Daughter of shipbroker George Washington Sandell (who died in 1945 at 93), Miss Sandell bought 44 Winn Road in 1923 and lived there until 1971, when she removed to flats in Westwood Road. That year a block of flats in The Parkway, Bassett, was named Sandell Court, in compliment to her — primarily for her work in preserving and popularising the historical heritage of the town she loved and served in so many ways. Besides her numerous books, articles and lectures on local history, she maintained a wide range of interests right up to her death in 1974 at 83. She was the leading spirit of the Friends of Old Southampton and the Southampton Commons and Public Lands Protection Society and was active in many other organisations, notably the Alliance Française, and as a co-opted member of the Public Libraries and Museums Committee. She was awarded the *Palmes Academiques* decoration by the French government in 1965 and an honorary M.A. of Southampton University the following year.

New College,

Westwood and
Brookvale Roads,
Southampton.

For the Daughters of Gentlemen.

THE SCHOOL is designed for Girls over seven years of age. Its aim is to develop the faculties, both intellectual and physical, of the Pupils, so as to enable them to continue their own education after they have left School, and to prepare them for the work of life.

NEW COLLEGE is situated in the best and most open part of Southampton (2½ miles from the Docks). It is not far from the Common, and is immediately neighboured by an extensive private park. A limited number of Boarders are received in the Headmistress' House, which adjoins the School. The Sanitary arrangements are inspected annually. The Pupils are prepared for Public Examinations, but the endeavour of those concerned in the conduct of the School is to make the work interesting and stimulating in itself, rather than to depend on examinations and prizes as motives to exertion. Every precaution is taken to avoid over-pressure. Physical Training is an important feature of the School life. Out-door games (cricket, tennis, hockey, etc.) are played under careful supervision.

Children of Parents residing abroad are received for the whole year, including the holidays, at special terms.

References are kindly permitted to:—Mrs. Creighton, Hampton Court Palace; The Right Rev. the Bishop of Leicester and Mrs. Clayton, The Precincts, Peterborough; E. A. Findlay, Esq., "Sandfield," Egerton Park, Rock Ferry, Cheshire; Major-General Byam, C.B., and Mrs. Byam, Barcaldine, Westwood Road, and others.

Principal - MISS ALLNUTT.

(Oxford Honour School of Classics. Sometime of the Princess Helena College), assisted by a fully Qualified Staff of

RESIDENT MISTRESSES AND VISITING PROFESSORS.

An advertisement for New College, soon after it was taken over by Miss Allnutt, about 1900.

Elsie Sandell is also remembered as the initiator of Southampton's D-Day embroidery, a remarkable co-operative project on which 76 ladies worked for three years — now displayed at the entrance to Southampton Central Library.

But what of the man who gave his name to the road where Elsie Sandell lived nearly half a century? One can now only speculate as to how William Winn was prompted to acquire the Westwood Park estate; he does not seem to have had any other connection with Southampton. Recent research (obligingly assisted by librarians and archivists of several London boroughs) has uncovered something of his background — but this makes it the more curious that such a man should have become involved in "up market" development of a Victorian suburb of Southampton.

William Winn was listed in Post Office directories of 1861-67 at 10 Campbell Terrace, Bow Road, Bromley. He served a term as one of the Bromley representatives on the Poplar District Board of Works in 1861-64 but was noticed only for not attending any of its 23 meetings held between June 1862 and April 1863! The page of the census schedule that should have recorded William Winn in 1861 is unfortunately lost but in 1871 he was noted as 40 years old, born in Limehouse and described as "lighterman and barge builder", a lodger at 16 St. Stephen's Road, Bow. This was rather grandly styled "Haddo House", in what was originally New Coborn Road, re-named in 1870, when the house was given a number. It was occupied by Mrs. Elizabeth Allsop, a widow of 60 in 1871, together with her nephew and niece William and Elizabeth Cross and their two young children. Mrs. Allsop kept two living-in servants. Mr. Winn was the only other member of the household. He was listed as married but there is no record of his wife, then or later, nor of any children — although William Henry Winn, living at Bexley between the wars, may have been a relative.

Documents of the 1880s for lease or sale of parts of the Westwood Park estate still styled him "William Winn Esq., of Haddo House, Bow, Middlesex". The 1881 census again listed him as a boarder (occupation "lighterman") in the house of Mrs. Allsop, where there were then two female visitors and one domestic servant. Winn was listed in Kelly's and Post Office directories at the same address through the 1880s but in 1894 George Winn was shown there — perhaps an error? In the Bow valuation list of 1890 William Winn was noted as the occupier of 16 St. Stephen's Road, with Mr. Cross as the owner — presumably Mrs. Allsop's nephew who was living in the house at the time of the 1871 census. At the next valuation in 1895 there was no entry for either occupier or owner, so the house was then empty. Perhaps William Winn had then died; born in 1831, he then would have been in his sixties. In 1894 he had sold out his remaining interest in Westwood Park to his Southampton agent and solicitor, Alexander Paris.

William Winn evidently prospered sufficiently in his barge business to amass capital for property deals, which put another Winn Road on the map in 1875 as part of the "Winn Estate" at Lee, Lewisham — although house building (on Garden Village lines) did not, in fact, proceed there until after the land had come into the hands of David Duncan (seemingly a London solicitor) and was put up for auction in 1910. Winn's Southampton links were still in evidence; the auctioneers were the Hampshire firm Richard Austin and Wyatt and the engineers and surveyors for the estate were Messrs. Lemon and Blizard — (Sir) James Lemon had acted for Winn at Westwood Park. Winn's Southampton agent and solicitors, Messrs. Paris, Smith and Randall, were also involved in the 1910 sale of the land at Lewisham which Winn had bought in the 1870s but never developed himself.

At Southampton in the 1880s, house building in Winn and Westwood Roads encouraged the separate development of land to the south, on the remainder of the old Bevois Mount estate acquired in 1844 by William Betts (see *Streets*, page 57). This enterprising contractor had financed his lavish improvements at Bevois Mount by selling off the southern part, built up as Bevois Town, but he over-reached himself and was obliged to dispose of Bevois Mount house and grounds in 1854, although he retained ownership of the area north of Avenue Road, up to the line of the future Gordon Avenue.

On his death in 1867 this passed to his heirs and trustees; when it became "ripe for development" they sold it (for £6,150, by conveyance dated January 8, 1886) to a local syndicate which brought together James Bailey of "Elmfield", Millbrook Road; Edward Brown, a successful butcher; and Charles Hardiman, an estate agent with offices in St. Mary's Road. Bailey rated an "esquire" and was evidently a gentleman with capital to invest. Edward Brown, who died at 77 in 1910, had built up a sizeable family business, with shops in Above Bar, Canal Walk, Shirley and Portswood. He served on the borough council, being sheriff in 1885-86, later an alderman and J.P.

William Winn helped the final development of the land adjoining his Westwood Park estate by agreeing to sell to the Bailey-Brown-Hardiman syndicate a strip of land which enabled houses with gardens to be built along the north side of Gordon Avenue, backing on to the properties on the south side of Westwood Road. This land was important to the local developers but of little value in itself to Winn, who conveyed it to them on January 28, 1886, for only £150.

The syndicate must have anticipated the formalities of this transaction and initiated its publicity, for the *Southampton Times* of January 9 announced the "Opening of the Gordon Avenue Estate": its reporter had seen the layout plans (tenders for road works and drainage had already been invited) and wrote of 150 houses intended to cover 18 acres — "all of a superior class of detached and semi-detached villa residences . . . the eligible and convenient situation will no doubt ensure a large and early demand for allotments". Good quality development was ensured by covenants in the building leases specifying that semi-detached villas should cost at least £600 a pair; they were supplemented by terraced houses along Livingstone Road, for which a minimum price of £150 applied.

The 1887 town directory recorded the first resident of Gordon Avenue — "J.J. Leach, illuminating artist" at "Fernside". The note "tenements now building" was expanded in the next edition of 1890 into a long list showing the road almost fully built up, likewise Livingstone Road running off it. Other entries indicated the close involvement of Brown and Hardiman in their property venture. Both were then established in new houses in New Alma Road, as the eastward extension of Alma Road from Cambridge Road to Portswood Road was then styled — Brown at "Hughenden" and Hardiman at 2 Spear Hall Villas.

This address carried the name of the "country house" built about 1765 in modest grounds within the area of the later Avenue, Portswood, Alma and Earl's Roads. In 1815 it was bought from "Thomas Williams of Southampton, woollen draper and mercer" by Charles Day, co-founder of the engineering and shipbuilding firm of Day, Summers and Co. Among later occupiers was George Lungley in the 1860s. He was a shipbuilder from Deptford who took over about 1856 John Rubie's yard on the Itchen, downstream of the Northam Iron Works; Lungley both built and owned several wooden sailing ships, particularly for the coastal coaling trade between Sunderland and Southampton. The last to live at Spear Hall were Mr. and Mrs. Selby, who died or left before 1890, by which time Spear Road had been laid out. Soon afterwards Spear Hall was demolished and the area (about two acres) was redeveloped with smaller houses, associated with the adjoining Gordon Avenue estate.

The choice of Gordon and Livingstone as names for the new roads of 1886 showed a nice combination of business acumen and Victorian sentiment, to provide a "good address" for suburban villas. Southampton could claim General Charles George Gordon as its own, since most of his comparatively short periods of home leave during the last twenty years of his adventurous life were spent in the town, at the home of his parents and eldest sister, 5 Rockstone Place. Their family tomb is in the Old Cemetery, off Hill Lane, under a tree by the Anglican chapel.

The father of "Chinese Gordon" was General William Gordon, who retired to Southampton about 1857, when he leased the house from the Misses Mary and Rebecca Toomer, two of the eight daughters and heirs of Edward Toomer (1765-1852). He was a successful High Street ironmonger who diversified into banking and property development, with his son Samuel as architect, responsible for building the Regency-style houses of Rockstone Place in 1833-41. After

The home of General Gordon – 5 Rockstone Place, Southampton – with the actor Robert Hardy at the window during filming of a BBC television programme about Gordon in 1982. (Photograph: Ivan Champion).

the death of his parents, Charles Gordon bought the house in 1874 for his sister, Mary Augusta, who lived there until she died in 1893, when it passed to her widowed sister, Helen. She remained there until her death in 1919, after which the house was sold and became offices. Acquired in 1968 by La Sainte Union College, "Gordon House" now accommodates its history department.

During most of his army career, Gordon was mistrusted in official circles as unconventional, even eccentric, by comparison with other officers of the day, who did not share his intense Christian beliefs and selfless austerity. While his military abilities were largely unharnessed by his own country, the circumstances of his death at Khartoum on January 26, 1885 instantly made him a national hero, acclaimed as martyr and elevated to the position of a warrior-saint. The emotional cult of Gordon's memory found expression in numerous memorials.

Southampton was quick off the mark with its monument, unveiled by the Mayor, James Bishop, on October 15. Made by Messrs. Garret and Haysom to the design of the Borough Surveyor, W.B.G. Bennett, it comprised a cross-surmounted cluster of four marble columns, based on a granite block bearing inscriptions noting the scenes of Gordon's military exploits and styling him "soldier, administrator, philanthropist". Raised on an earth mound, it became the main feature of the then new Queen's Park, which Mr. Bishop had formally opened on May 23 the same year. The park gave a new identity to the land known from medieval times as Porters Meadow, which the Corporation had taken over from Queen's College, Oxford.

A national memorial was erected in 1888 in Trafalgar Square — whence it was transferred to Victoria Embankment Gardens in 1953. This bronze statue shows Gordon in contemplative mood, standing with his arms folded, his head resting on his hand, as if in deep thought. He holds a Bible; under his arm is the cane that served as his "wand" while leading men in battle; across his side are slung his binoculars; his left foot rests on a damaged mortar. Charity, Justice, Fortitude and Faith are exemplified as the virtues associated with Gordon. A more elaborate replica was erected in 1889 in a very different "Victorian" setting — 10,000 miles away, in the heart of Melbourne.

These memorials were created by Sir William Hamo Thornycroft (1850-1925), who was also responsible for several other famous London statues (including Cromwell and Gladstone) as well as that of King Alfred, set up at Winchester in 1901. His parents were likewise distinguished sculptors but the family name is today familiar primarily through their eldest son, Sir John Isaac Thornycroft (1843-1928), the naval architect who started his shipyard at Chiswick in 1866 and moved his operations in 1904 to Woolston. He has a modest street memorial in Thornycroft Avenue, tucked away behind Victoria Road. It was built up in 1910-14, just before the outbreak of the war in which the Woolston yard made a vital contribution to British naval power

(More about General Gordon's Southampton connections, the BBC television programme which included scenes with Robert Hardy at 5 Rockstone Place, and Gordon memorials and mementoes can be read in articles in *Hampshire* magazine, June and November 1981 and January 1985.)

Southampton shared the national rejoicing when Lord Kitchener's forces avenged Gordon by re-conquering the Sudan, defeating the Dervishes at Omdurman and re-occupying Khartoum in 1898. Pride in these victories quickly found expression in the commemorative naming of new streets — Omdurman and Khartoum Roads, along with Nile Road, in Highfield and Kitchener Road in Portswood. The latter was flanked by Sirdar Road, taking Kitchener's title as commander of the Egyptian army. East of the Itchen, Sholing was also given its own little Sirdar Road but in 1954 this was re-named Viceroy Road to eliminate duplication after that year's extension of the borough boundary.

Opposite: Dr. Livingstone's remains at Southampton: Procession to the railway station. (Illustrated London News, April 25, 1874).

REGISTERED AT THE GENERAL POST-OFFICE FOR TRANSMISSION ABROAD.

No. 1809.—VOL. LXIV. SATURDAY, APRIL 25, 1874. WITH EXTRA SUPPLEMENT {SIXPENCE. By Post, 6½d.

DR. LIVINGSTONE'S REMAINS AT SOUTHAMPTON; PROCESSION TO THE RAILWAY STATION.

The other great Victorian hero, Dr. David Livingstone, the missionary-explorer who spent nearly half his life in "darkest Africa", had a Southampton connection only after his death, when his body was brought ashore at the Royal Pier on April 15, 1874. The *Southampton Times* considered that "Southampton did quite as much honour to itself as it did to the memory of Dr. Livingstone by the reception which it gave to his remains", due to the Mayor, Edwin Jones (of department store fame) who "determined upon maturing such plans as should reflect credit on the community".

As soon as he learned that the P. & O. steamer *Malwa* carrying the body would call at Southampton, he secured the agreement of the Foreign Office and Livingstone's family that it should be landed at Southampton and arranged appropriate ceremonies. Livingstone's father-in-law Dr. Moffatt and H.M. Stanley were among the reception party taken out to the *Malwa*, ahead of the coffin being landed at the Royal Pier. Thence an impressive procession accompanied the hearse through High Street, Bernard Street and Oxford Street — lined by mourning thousands below shuttered windows and half-masted flags — to the Terminus station. There the coffin was placed on a special train to London, to lie in state at the premises of the Royal Geographical Society until the burial service at Westminster Abbey — which the mayor and his reception committee attended by the Society's special invitation.

This impressive statue of General Gordon by Sir William Hamo Thornycroft has stood in the centre of Melbourne since 1889. (Photograph: Tessa Leonard).

Acknowledgements

This book incorporates material from some of the weekly series of articles published in 1980-87 by the *Southern Evening Echo,* to which grateful acknowledgement is made. These original explorations of aspects of local history and biography have since been revised and extended, thanks partly to readers and correspondents who kindly provided additional information. I hope they will excuse me if I do not name them all.

I am particularly obliged to Mr. R.J. Newcombe and Mr. J.C. Davies for their contributions to the biography of J.W. Newcombe; Mr. C. Wesley for information about his grandfather, C.H. Meadows; and Mrs. I.M. Priestley and Mr. G.R. Warren for recollections of their childhood years at "The Vinery".

Detailed references and lengthy bibliography would overload this book. It will be evident from the text that I have drawn extensively on the resources of the Local Studies section of Southampton Central Library — for books, newspapers and other printed materials, census schedules and maps — and the Civic Record Office, for a wide range of documents, including Corporation records, rate books, deeds, sales particulars, transcripts of parish registers, tithe redemption schedules and maps and miscellaneous papers.

Like every student of local history, I am indebted to previous writers but wherever possible I have sought original sources and contemporary references to check and supplement their accounts.

For research facilities and courteous assistance over a number of years, I am grateful to Local Studies librarian Miss G. Forrest, the City Archivist, Miss S.D. Thomson, and their colleagues. My thanks are likewise due to members of the City Museums Service for valued help, particularly with illustrations.

INDEX

This index gives the key words for streets, roads etc, named after or connected with the people referred to in this book, also other persons or subjects mentioned.